SAVING YOUR
A$$ets

SAVING YOUR
A$$ets

Asset Protection for Texans
(and Maybe Everyone Else)

Henry W. Simon Jr.

BROWN BOOKS
PUBLISHING GROUP

Saving Your Assets

Brown Books Publishing Group
16250 Knoll Trail Drive, Suite 205
Dallas, Texas 75248
www.BrownBooks.com
(972) 381-0009

A New Era in Publishing™

ISBN 978-1-61254-164-8
LCCN 2014931886

Printed in the United States
10 9 8 7 6 5 4 3 2 1

This book is dedicated to all those successful individuals who have worried about the security of their personal assets but who have believed the subject to be too complicated or expensive to pursue.

⇠ CONTENTS ⇢

~ INTRODUCTION ~

Blessed with Exciting Times

Jack Benny, the late, great comedian who in character was stingy, performed certain pattern-comedy routines that people loved and laughed at, no matter how many times they witnessed his acts. One of his best routines was a skit in which he encountered a thief holding a revolver who accosted him. The thief demanded, "Your money or your life." Benny said nothing. The thief raised his voice, "I said your money or your life. Are you deaf?" Jack Benny again hesitated, and then he said, "I'm thinking, I'm thinking."

Your wealth is important, particularly to you. Most likely, you worked very hard to accumulate it. It's the key to your retirement, or if you have been very fortunate, it is the key to a very pleasant lifestyle at any age. You don't want to lose it, and you certainly don't want to lose it as the result of a single, isolated event that wreaks devastating financial results.

The message of this book is that a properly designed, legal framework, completed before financial disaster, is your best defense against ever needing to consider bankruptcy. Developing a careful plan for your assets will give you the ability to protect your holdings from any initial attack and the opportunity to make the best arrangement with your personal creditors. If, God forbid, you bet the farm and suffer an overwhelming personal financial loss, which I hope to show you how to avoid, you can still, with some attention to detail, live well using your protected assets. My goal is to provide the legal background necessary to demonstrate the need for asset protection and to point you in the best direction to design the right plan for you.

When considering your options following or in the midst of a personal financial disaster, the first thought or maybe the second, after considering hiking into Patagonia, is bankruptcy. That's entirely appropriate. Bankruptcy provides a mechanism to free a debtor from the continuing harassment of his current creditors or at least most of them. The price, quite intentionally, is very high and, if the debtor has any extensive assets, very expensive. The usual debtor emerges from bankruptcy only with the assets that are exempt from the claims of creditors under the exemption laws of his or her state of residence.

At its best, bankruptcy can bring some peace of mind because it stops harassment by creditors; however, only a competent bankruptcy lawyer can advise you properly concerning the bankruptcy options. There is some give and take, but federal law affords bankruptcy as a voluntary option. If you think you need to file for bankruptcy, obtain professional advice and think the decision through thoroughly.

Considering bankruptcy can be avoided if you protect your assets before a crisis. Most vendors of advice want to sell you or enable some affiliate to sell you a package of asset-protection documents. I don't want to do that. My reluctance is based on my experience in the field of combat between those who owe a lot of money and those who want to lay claim to it. In my trade, the former are debtors and the latter are creditors. For reasons that will be explored in this book, most folks do not need documentary asset protection, but those who do need a personalized plan tailored to the laws of their state of residence and accomplished through the services of a skilled lawyer who practices law in that state. All effective asset protection is local because it tracks the advantages of the laws in your state of residence.

I authored this guide because I believe I have valuable experience that I would enjoy sharing with you. I am a lawyer, practicing in Fort Worth, Texas. I graduated from Yale University and the University Of Texas Law School. I became an insolvency lawyer in the late 1970s because clients with those concerns hired me. The courts in the Southwest were exploding with insolvency matters—both bankruptcy courts and state courts—because the prices of oil and gas soared and then crashed, and other large enterprises were jeopardized.

I came by lawyering naturally. My grandfather was a lawyer. My father and uncle, with whom I practiced, were noted, skilled lawyers. My uncle had two sons, Richard and James, each a noted and skilled lawyer. Additionally, my first cousin, James F. Simon, served for many years as dean of the City University of New York School of Law and has authored several acclaimed books on both law and history. My wife, Karen, and I have two sons, Robert and Jeffrey, both noted and skilled lawyers. Some in Fort Worth might say that the male members of the Simon family do not know how to make an honest living.

One of life's blessings is to live in exciting times. For eighty years, bankruptcy practitioners operated under the Bankruptcy Act of 1898, a somewhat opaque and confusing statute. In 1978, Congress repealed the statute and enacted the United States Bankruptcy Code to make reorganization under Chapter 11 a better option. The bankruptcy judges in North Central Texas, who were amazingly talented, wanted debtors to file in their jurisdiction and reorganize successfully. Business was great for bankruptcy firms that contained lawyers with some business background.

My firm represented a class of public debt holders in the Braniff Airlines bankruptcy, a class of preferred shareholders in the 7–11 convenience store case, a former director in the Zales Jewelry case, English/Scottish pension funds that had invested $125 million in the Amarex/Hefner cases in Oklahoma City, the Official Creditors Committee in Sunshine Mining in Idaho, as well as Furr's Foods, a large west Texas grocery retailer, as counsel to the debtor until it was sold, under a bankruptcy plan, to Toom's Market, a German company. The big one was really two assignments—we were debtor's counsel to Placid Oil Company, owned by three of the H. L. Hunt first-family siblings trusts and, after that, co-counsel to Nelson Bunker Hunt in his contentious but successful personal bankruptcy.

I have met many of America's more original financial thinkers. There were some who were wrong, some who were on the right track before their time, and some who were vindicated in the end. None was or is more memorable than Nelson Bunker Hunt.

Nelson Bunker Hunt is the son of the legendary Texas oilman H. L. Hunt. Bunker has been the subject of a huge amount of personal publicity in magazines including the Sunday supplement to the *New York Times*, in books, and in countless newspapers. I met him as a final result of the economic disaster that he and his brother Herbert suffered when they tried unsuccessfully to corner the silver market. The Commodity Futures Trading Commission abruptly changed its rules regarding silver future holdings, leaving the brothers with huge, inescapable losses. They covered their positions, expensively, by causing their family owned oil company, Placid Oil, to borrow enough money to cover their losses. Oil prices dropped precipitously in the 1980s, and Placid entered Chapter 11 bankruptcy in Dallas. The Hunts' original bankruptcy counsel was forced to withdraw, and our Fort Worth firm was engaged.

There are many available descriptions of Bunker Hunt; some are very negative. I never saw that side. Mr. Hunt was always courteous to me although many of the intricacies of the bankruptcy process bored him. They did not bore his brother, William Herbert Hunt, who has an excellent aptitude for detail and quickly learned the process and its procedures.

Bunker Hunt was not a helpless debtor, despite huge losses. He was the beneficiary of a large trust established in 1935 by his father and thus was able to pay any personal expenses. Whether he could pay for his grand business ambitions was another matter, but he had great faith in the holdings of Placid Oil and wanted to be proven right. Ultimately he was. Sort of below the surface of his more sensational activities as a silver speculator and owner of world-class horses, he is a talented non-professional oil finder. He has discovered, among many others of lesser size, a huge field in Florida and a gigantic field in Libya. He also had ideas about deep-water production. When Placid failed to produce natural gas after drilling a test well in the Gulf of Mexico,

Mr. Hunt turned to Placid's holdings in the North Sea between the Netherlands and the British Isles. Contrary to all common wisdom, he convinced Placid's management to drill a gas well in a lightly regarded block in the Dutch-assigned section of the North Sea. He also championed a very different method of "completion": mechanical procedures to induce gas production. He was right—very, very right. A huge discovery paved the way for Placid to reorganize successfully and repay more than a billion dollars to creditors.

What does this bit of history have to do with asset protection? Here's the answer: Bunker Hunt had the luxury of time. His personal circumstances granted him protection from immediate family need, allowing him time to explore his options. Even if you don't own oil concessions, you also need time and relief from the pressures of creditors in order to right your ship.

Even if you lack the skill of Nelson Bunker Hunt and the range of assets upon which to practice, the longer your creditors have to wait for their money, and the more money they have spent trying to collect, the more reasonable they will become. A competent asset-protection plan will provide you with the necessary time and disincentives. That's what I am preaching—a stitch in time saves nine.

What lawyers really like most is to give people meaningful and valuable advice. At least that's what I like, and that's what I hope to do in this book.

— 1 —

Gone to the Lone Star State: Asset Protection and Texas Exemptions

This book is titled *Saving Your A$$ets: Asset Protection for Texans (and Maybe Everyone Else)*. Why mention only Texas? In large measure because I live here and always have, except for going to college in Connecticut and working in Washington, DC. In other words, I'm familiar with Texas law and practice; however, the general themes are common to the laws of all other states. Any skilled lawyer can advise you on the specific laws of your state of residence. If you don't like the specific laws of your state, move to Texas.

The goals of asset protection are to make your personal assets less available to your grasping creditors. I assume that you may at least contemplate suffering a large economic loss; we cannot deny risk. I further assume that it would be a great inconvenience to you to cover in cash all that you owe. You want and need a better alternative than turning your pockets inside out and handing over all your money. The primary defense against creditors is time, time for creditors to spend money chasing you and then become tired of the chase. Time is also needed for you to rearrange or improve your economic circumstances, which will enable you to make a satisfactory deal so you can put all this unpleasantness behind you.

These are litigious times. You should assess your vulnerability to litigation. Recall that the first rule of elective litigation is to sue someone with money. You must decide if you are such a person. Re-evaluating your net worth regularly is a good idea. Consider the present value of your investments and any inherited assets. Many financial experts suggest the standard for wealth today is a net worth of $1 million. If you are a resident of Texas, I consider you wealthy enough to need an asset protection plan if you have a substantial net worth of around $500,000 in excess of the value of your Texas homestead and all of your qualified retirement plans. If your homestead exemption is limited by the laws of another state or by a less than complete holding period for federal bankruptcy use, make those adjustments to err on the side of caution.

A little Texas history helps explain the statutes in Texas that protect debtors. Like all states, Texas has its legends and tall tales, but unlike most states, the legends and tall tales in Texas are true. No tales are taller than the stories about the Alamo. What does the Alamo have to do with asset protection? It all goes back to the nineteenth-century folk hero with the coonskin cap, Davy Crockett.

Davy Crockett, beloved by all Texans and many Disney viewers, was broke and owed a lot of money to creditors when he left Tennessee to go west to Texas. At his departure, he told his creditors, "You all can go to hell; I'm going to Texas." This was a wise choice economically. The brand new Republic of Texas had been settled and organized by more than a few folks who had left creditors behind in other places. To ensure that those creditors did not pursue them to Texas, they enacted laws that were immensely favorable to debtors, leaving most creditors without any effective remedy, even if they chased their debtor to Texas. Davy's economic plan was sound. Unfortunately, his military mission was doomed, and he died, valiantly in the minds of all true Texans, at the Alamo. No deal is perfect.

Davy is gone, but Texas retains the tradition of being a debtor-friendly state in one important respect—the famous homestead exemption, available to every resident of Texas, single or married, in an unlimited amount subject to certain residency requirements. Texas is joined by only Florida in its homestead exemption leniency, although Kansas is not far behind.

Assume that, while solvent, and without specific knowledge of any devastating financial clouds hanging over, you pay $1 million for a Texas homestead, a residence in Fort Worth near Texas Christian University, a much-beloved university with a super football program. This is a nice area where there is a good chance for appreciation. You now have a Texas homestead, but you must live there three years and eight months to have full protection of the value of your home in bankruptcy. Obviously if you financed your purchase by putting a mortgage on the house, known in Texas as a deed of trust, the mortgage holder must be paid if you sell the house. To stay in the house, you have to pay the mortgage lender and the property taxes, but your other creditors have no right to sell your homestead or put a lien on it to collect your debts to them.

If you are actually facing a financial crisis and bankruptcy is a possibility, pay off your mortgage. Your cash might be vulnerable to creditors; the equity in your house is not.

You may be wondering if you should sell stocks and your expensive toys like cars and airplanes to pay off your mortgage. The answer is yes, but it takes some knowledge and guidance because of a new provision of the Bankruptcy Code. Section 522(o) may limit your homestead exemption if you bought the house and paid off the loan on the property with an intent to hinder, delay, or defraud a creditor by converting non-exempt property into an exempt homestead. If you develop good asset protection practices, you will never have to consider bankruptcy, although you need to know a little about it. Here's what you need to do first to begin to protect your assets:

» Live in the Lone Star State or, at present, Florida, although several other states are improving their homestead protections.

» Acquire a homestead that will likely appreciate over time.

» Pay off any mortgage as soon as you can.

» If you have to pay off your mortgage now because the wolves are baying outside your door, do so with legal help.

» Although this discussion of asset protection opened with Texas's homestead exemptions, there are many more exemptions in Texas, and they too are favorable when compared to most states. You must remember, though, that the exemptions apply without challenge only if the assets were acquired and paid for before storm clouds appeared on the economic horizon.

There is a reason for this close drill on Texas's statutory exemptions. If you are not now or in the future engaged in any venture that might result in liability on contractual debt, you are not in a divorcing mood, and you don't drink and drive, you may conclude that Texas's or another state's exemptions, when understood, are sufficient so that you don't need a formal asset protection plan. It may well be true that your lifestyle is less risky than many others, but you cannot control serious illness—yours or one that afflicts your family—and, as we shall see, serious illness presents a financial risk that most of us do not yet understand. And there are other options, so be prudent and protect yourself properly, at least to the full extent of state law.

Texas divides its exemptions between the very helpful homestead, including funeral plots, real estate exemptions, and personal property exemptions. They change occasionally. Here's what the exemptions are as of June 2013:

» Tangible personal property, excluding cash, in the amounts of $60,000 for a family or $30,000 for a single adult

» All current wages for personal services, except for enforcement of court-ordered child-support payments

» All doctor-prescribed health aids

» Alimony, support, or separate maintenance

» A Bible or any other religious book of prayer, except in favor of a lessor's right to seize property to remedy a breach of lease

» Unpaid commissions for personal services, not to exceed 25 percent of the $60,000 (or $30,000) limitation previously discussed

» A long list of household items (food, furniture, farm and ranching implements, clothes, jewelry subject to a 25 percent of allowed personal value limitation, guns, sports equipment, a bunch of farm animals, and household pets). Note: the treatment of expensive computer and related equipment is still being argued as to the limitation to be applied.

» A lovely, unlimited exemption for IRAs, 401Ks, annuities, and other retirement plans of almost every type so long as the plan is tax qualified under federal law. The legislature intended to leave necessary retirement plans unaffected by creditors' claims.

» Once again, however, allow reason to temper your most inventive ideas. If you put the money in after you already owe the creditor, it is vulnerable, but the test is favorable. Creditors must prove that you knew the creditors were unlikely to be paid. This is more an application of the doctrine of fraudulent transfer than an intrusion into the sanctity of Texas exemptions. That specific concept is embodied in the statute as "Transfer of Nonexempt Property." The then-acknowledged debtor cannot change the character of his property from non-exempt, and therefore available to the creditor, to exempt, and hence unavailable, at least not without a fight. As you might imagine, there has been plenty of litigation over how to characterize transfers by a debtor, but while the cases turn on their individual facts, the concept is not hard to understand. No one should be able to make non-exempt property into exempt property after he knows he can't pay his creditors.

On a comparative basis, the Texas exemptions are very good, better in my experience than those of any other state. That's the reason we discuss them so fully.

Given that the Texas exemptions are the most generous in the country, there will be those who will try to take a bit of an advantage. A case, still laughed over, occurred in the Fort Worth bankruptcy court many years ago. On the bench sat John Calvin Ford, a truly remarkable judge, known not only for his acumen, which was significant, but also for that special wisdom that sets the great judges apart. The case before Judge Ford involved a doctor from the then-small, neighboring town of Burleson, Texas, just south of Fort Worth on Interstate 35.

The doctor had engaged in risky investing, lost his bets, and owed a lot of money—about $500,000—to a couple of banks and one rich individual. The doctor did not wish to pay his creditors anything, and his bankruptcy papers declared that there would be no distribution to creditors. The reason was that the doctor had carefully prepared for bankruptcy. At that time, there was no significant length of residency required to support a homestead exemption. The doctor and his wife had acquired for cash an expensive home, but that was not the end of the doctor's planning.

Marching carefully down the list of available exempt property, the doctor had acquired for cash a new vehicle for himself and his wife. Per their bankruptcy disclosure, each drove a very expensive, over-the-road truck diesel-power unit. Today this would be a Kenworth or Peterbilt tractor at a cost of three times any passenger vehicle.

Following the agricultural exemptions, the doctor had acquired two show horses at high prices. The gun exemptions were filled by expensive, jeweled, antique firearms. Each other relevant category was also the subject of a very-expensive purchase, obviously in contemplation of filing.

Judge Ford listened quietly to the evidence detailing all these purchases. There were fraudulent transfer implications, but it was not clear that purchases of exempt property could be avoided, and the federal limitation that now may erode the full homestead exemption in bankruptcy, had not then been passed into bankruptcy law.

The judge continued listening very carefully, and when the doctor and his attorney had said all, he finally spoke. He said that every rule can be broken by abuse and that reasonable people could differ to a point but that there's a point beyond that when good faith was in contest and had to be evaluated. He then added that the doctor could not pass a good-faith test. He concluded, though, that the doctor was not any kind of wrongdoer because he had fully explained his activities. Ultimately, the judge lowered the dollar value of the more egregious exemptions, leaving the doctor with an obligation to pay his creditors $125,000, upon which he would achieve his discharge from his debts, the goal of every individual who files bankruptcy.

He made his final pronouncement, "Doc, you just sliced the ham too thin."

Everyone walked out of the courtroom pretty much satisfied. There's a moral to this story: take every advantage that state law provides, but do so within the realm of reason.

— 2 —

All That Glitters Is Not at Risk:
The Individual Need for an
Asset Protection Plan

Unless there are very special circumstances, it is unlikely that anyone with assets much under $500,000, exclusive of homestead and retirement set asides, would be an appropriate candidate for formal asset protection, which is only acquired at some price for the services of knowledgeable counsel. The following stories of people's financial situations are offered to help you determine whether you or someone you know and love should be considering an asset protection plan. Only after that question is answered either "yes" or "probably," shall we then proceed to determine what kind of asset protection plan will be needed and under what circumstances.

The first subject of inquiry is a lovely seventy-five-year-old widow who received her share of one-half of her late husband's community property, which resulted in her ownership, free and clear, of her $750,000 home in the Lakewood section of Dallas. She owns a nice car and very nice and extremely well-selected jewelry. She receives full Social Security and installment payments on her husband's insurance. In addition, she has financial assets in excess of $1.5 million that are managed by her son-in-law, a noted investment advisor at Morgan Stanley. Five days a week and a few nights as well, she plays duplicate bridge. Often she dines with her children and her grandchildren.

Is this nice and somewhat wealthy lady in need of an intricate asset protection plan? No, she is not. She is not likely to take any significant financial risks, and she benefits from having competent, loving advisors. She may safely stick to bridge.

Charles's story is very different. He is a fifty-two-year-old-happily-married man who lives in Austin. Charles rents a fantastic condo on the lake; he and his wife drive large and expensive Mercedes automobiles; and they own and enjoy all of the necessities and expensive toys of the Austin lifestyle. Charles manages a hedge fund of modest size, but the participants of the fund are his old classmates from the Harvard Business School, and the fund operates conservatively but with considerable success. He invests privately in European equities and is fairly conservative in his investment choices. Charles also has $2 million in personal cash in very conservative investments.

Unfortunately, Charles has a blind side—his brother Fred. Charles has agreed, although he certainly should not have, to back his brother in a can't-miss reinvention of the Bobby Jones "Calamity Jane" putter—"no more three putts guaranteed!" Does Charles need asset protection? Yes, he does because he has very little exempt property, and he is about to take some risks. He finds himself in need of asset protection despite the fact that even if the financial risks of his own enterprises decline, so long as he has not borrowed against them, one may assume that they will recover under good stewardship. Everything is fine until Charles guarantees his brother's financing, which will enable the worldwide rollout of the new Calamity Jane putter. That single act, signing a guarantee for a business he does not control, moves him to a person in high need of asset protection.

Another potential candidate for asset protection is a man we'll call Big Time or BT. He is a true athletic hero, one of the best fielding shortstops in the last fifteen years. BT played in four All-Star games and in three World Series, was twice a winner, and holds a few records still on baseball's books. This guy could go to his left, go to his right, go in the hole. He had an arm like a bazooka. Today BT lives in a 10,000-square-foot house in Houston and owns five cars and a beautiful powerboat yacht in a marina near Galveston. BT has $12 million in the bank and no significant liabilities. Does a fellow with no liabilities and $12 million in the bank need asset protection? You bet he does, big time, and right now. Why is that? Because BT's big earning days are over. The sports spotlight is now cast on other players, but BT maintains and retains a very expensive lifestyle. Troubles lie ahead.

If BT runs to type, like other once-great athletes, he will invest in a series of speculative enterprises. Financial finesse is not what enabled BT to make those memorable throws. Memories are short—the adjustment is hard from being a media darling to "That guy looks familiar. Who was he?"

Based on sad, true stories, BT is not very far away from losing a great deal (or all) of his money in a series of disastrous investments promoted by others, generally operated by others, with the exception of a few star turns by BT. He is in no position to correctly evaluate investments, nor is he in any position to grade the performance of his friends as economic partners. He doesn't have the training, and the people who hang around him are there mostly for his society and his money. None of these people hold MBAs. So, at recognized risk, BT very badly needs a competent asset protection plan that he can develop satisfactorily under the laws of Texas.

Along the same lines as BT, Charles is also at risk financially, but in his case, it is due to his entirely understandable affection for his younger brother Fred. As the older brother, Charles primarily raised, supported, and put Fred through several fine schools. Fred obtained neither a degree nor a great deal of basic economic learning. He pretty much relied on the skill and the financial resources of his brother who cannot say no to him. But Charles knows his own weakness. Accordingly he is very nervous about his support of Fred's new venture, and he is thinking very hard about his personal circumstances.

He already asked if the bank providing the financing will limit his personal liability to $200,000. They said no, or at least that's what his brother told him. Charles knows enough to fear the consequences of an unlimited guarantee, but as of now, he just doesn't know how to tell his brother no.

What to do? Charles does a little reading. And then he carefully explains what he is about to do to his wife Barbara who loves Charles very much but deeply distrusts his brother. She fully shares his concerns, and the two of them decide to try to protect themselves. Charles's best friend and frequent golf partner is a non-practicing lawyer who serves as head of the land title department of an oil and gas exploration company. Lawyers work for him. He asks around. He, Charles, and Barbara get together, make decisions, and start the process of protecting their assets.

Charles and Barbara begin by obtaining the advice of one of Austin's smartest residential real estate brokers. They want a house that will appreciate in value. Because they are decisive and can close immediately, a great opportunity presents itself. They buy a $1.75-million house in the West Lake Hills section of Austin, paying

$1 million down. Charles and Barbara initiate and add to their individual tax-sheltered retirement plans. They receive assurance that these plans are exempt from the claims of creditors.

Charles and Barbara are advised by their trusted friend to engage a specialized asset protection lawyer, but they declined. They were reluctant to tell a stranger, even a lawyer who is required to maintain confidentiality, that they fear the golf venture will fail, and that they are protecting themselves. For this reason, the leading counsel in the field of asset protection in Austin remains a total stranger to Charles and Barbara. They don't want to widen the circle of those informed. Their decision is made. Charles and Barbara, with a little help from their friends, decide to do their personal asset protection plan themselves.

Charles intentionally delays the date on which he is to sign the guarantee. He has unexpected trips and is closing two big deals. He'll get by the bank and sign but not today.

Charles executes a gift deed transfer to Barbara covering all of her personal jewelry, furs, and all collectibles such as art, antiques, sculptures, gold and silver serving pieces, and some securities. The document is properly filed for record with the county clerk of Travis County, Texas. The securities are transferred with Medallion Guarantees that are required to complete the transfer of registered stocks.

Charles and Barbara then partition or divide all the rest of their property except the homestead and the two exempt cars. He owns one-half, she owns one-half. And, as you have guessed by now, Barbara will not sign the guarantee.

Finally Charles executes an agreement with his partners, giving them an unconditional right to purchase his interest in the private equity firm, which is, and always was, a limited liability company.

Having accomplished all these tasks, Charles delivers to the bank a personal financial statement titled "Combined Assets/Liabilities of Charles and Barbara Smith." It shows a lot of net worth, no then-existing liabilities except a home mortgage and a substantial income. He doesn't give the banker much time to review the document because he is conveniently on his way out of town. He signs the unlimited guarantee on the bank form, and the bank then funds the loan. The Calamity Jane Putter Company is in business on Charles's credit.

The Calamity Jane putter was well-named. Its operation is a calamity. The Korean factory engaged to manufacture the putter has never made a similar golf club. The putter heads themselves are not uniform. The face of the putter gives off a discordant thump when the club is employed. "Not to worry," says Fred. All the manufacturing problems will be solved. Surprisingly, they were. The Koreans re-designed their equipment and produced a uniform, nice-looking golf club. There was only one problem—what worked for Bobby Jones on very slow Bermuda greens seventy or so years ago does not work well on today's very tight, slick grasses where just a little wiggle or wobble will ruin the stroke. That's the reason the anchor putter came into existence. The anchoring prevents most of the undesirable wiggle.

In short, the Calamity Jane was a failure, exactly as Charles and Barbara had feared. The bank, exercising horrible judgment but knowing it had Charles's guarantee, kept lending. The bank lost, with interest and fees, $975,000. And then a small event of good fortune appeared on the horizon. Fred, who was foolish but not criminal, found a buyer in Indonesia for the inventory. He found someone with credentials who believed that additional weighting behind the putter head would do wonders. Everyone hoped so, but the better news was that the loss chargeable under Charles's guarantee was reduced to $798,000. This is no cause to celebrate, but it was a better outcome.

The bank or rather their lawyers wrote letters and then came calling. "Please pay us now," they demanded. By now, Charles had hired a highly competent insolvency lawyer. The meetings were courteous but testy, then intense. The bank's lawyers learned about the affairs of Charles and Barbara as they had every right to do. What they learned did not make their day.

Charles and Barbara had broken no laws. They were not insolvent when they gifted and partitioned nor when they bought an expensive, exempt-under-Texas-law homestead. And they are not insolvent today. Husbands and wives can partition community property. Charles's partners have and need a preferential right to acquire his interest in the business.

What about the strangely titled financial statement? The financial statement correctly described the combined assets of Charles and Barbara—all true—every word of it. Ask no questions, expect no answers. One final issue to consider was whether Charles knew Fred's enterprise would fail? He did not. Fears and doubts are not the same as knowing.

Charles settled with the bank for $200,000, which is more than his new lawyer advised him to pay. He replied that he had offered a $200,000 guarantee that he would have paid immediately if called upon. He rightfully considers himself a man of integrity. So he saved some serious money, and he now believes Fred has really learned his lesson. Maybe yes, maybe no, but Charles has learned his—finally.

That's pure self-help by a very smart Texas couple. A properly constructed asset protection plan is far, far better. It's better because signing a guarantee is the only unfortunate financial event in which the debtor controls the calendar. He can refuse to sign, or he can delay signing. There is little to no controlling when your spouse files for divorce or when you or a loved one are involved in a horrible car wreck, particularly one accompanied by alcohol. Tort cases rarely occur at the best of times and usually do occur at the worst of times. There is no time to design or carry out the several phases, along with legal documentation, that are necessary in an endeavor more formal than the one Charles and Barbara undertook.

Beginning an asset protection plan on your own is kind of like going on a miserable diet and losing a bunch of weight. The diet is hard to start and even harder to complete. And, even if you do it and find happily that you don't need it, you still feel miserable. Many married couples do not get along as well as Charles and Barbara. And your assets change, sometimes a lot, almost without realization. Charles and Barbara's endeavor created a static plan with disclosed assets. It can and likely will become obsolete. If you try to model your asset protection plan off of theirs, it likely won't be fully serviceable when you need it. But for a couple of amateurs—hats off to Charles and Barbara!

How Tall Is Your Cotton?
Evaluating Your Circumstances

Most Americans do not need formal asset protection. By formal asset protection, I mean a personal plan and a management regime tailored only for you. But if you have read this far, probably you are in the process of figuring out whether you need a personal plan and, if so, who should prepare it and at what cost.

It isn't hard to isolate the first criteria. Do you have substantial assets to protect? We'll assume you do or think you may. We accept that those assets are very important to you, but if they amount to less than $500,000, excluding your home, cars, and qualified retirement plans, as we have said, you probably don't need a formal asset protection plan (APP). But if you reasonably anticipate acquiring new wealth, the time to create your personal APP is now.

In fact, you will probably not be served well by acquiring some sort of a standardized product, maybe one publically advertised on the Internet or by written solicitation. In large cities, you may be invited to a free dinner that involves listening to a one-size-fits-all pitch. It doesn't because in this particular field, the ongoing process is more important than any one-time product. You need the tools, but they don't help much if you don't know how to use them.

It is easy to understand why a financial high roller needs a dandy APP. We all know the stories about those fallen-from-high estates. But are there other financial reverses that are common enough to require evaluation? Unfortunately, there are. In my experience, the most disheartening financial experiences are listed and explained below:

- Divorce
- Driving mishaps, particularly when accompanied by alcohol
- Tort claims, exclusive of driving errors
- Guarantees of commercial indebtedness
- Medical costs as a special form of guarantee

Divorce, especially an unfortunate, untimely divorce, will result in the division of your assets, generally leaving one spouse with the non-liquid assets while the other gets the benefit of the assets that he or she can use immediately to relocate and provide for the children. Most people who undergo an unpleasant divorce, particularly without the benefit of a fully adequate pre-nuptial agreement, come away with personal fortunes significantly reduced. Whether it is true to that extreme or not, someone's personal fortune will be reduced, and he or she will be more vulnerable to the vicissitudes of ordinary business activity. After going through an expensive divorce, it is not a joyous thought to having to engage another set of lawyers.

Driving mishaps can happen to anyone who drives automobiles, SUVs, and light trucks with varying degrees of skill. Unfortunately as you get older, the basic skills needed for safe driving tend to erode. Mishaps occur and legal responsibility follows, sometimes in the form of lawsuits alleging that you or someone you allowed to drive your vehicle drove unsafely or should never have been allowed to drive. And, once again, because the truth hurts, there are times when we drive, particularly after drinking or becoming fatigued, when we just should not have done so. Motor vehicles can cause great harm and, regrettably, death. Under a variety of circumstances, including just failure to renew your insurance, large claims arise. If you take the matter to a jury, you may be very disappointed in the result. Asset protection is very, very helpful in these circumstances.

Many tort claims are totally unrelated to driving or allowing someone allegedly unqualified to drive your car. There are a variety of legal claims—some quite historical and others of the recent vintage—which may arise against you: slander; wrongful dismissal of a business employee; tortious, i.e., unlawful interference with another's business; violation of fiduciary obligations, if you act as a formal or informal trustee in managing someone else's money; and unfortunately, a host of claims that may arise from within your family, particularly if you are clearly the most financially successful member.

Most people are well aware of the disparities in the outcomes of tort litigation—suits not only about personal injury but also about economic losses and claims for punitive damages arising from business transactions. Different judges and different juries will reach sometimes spectacularly different results when determining seemingly similar "facts" in economic litigation. That is unavoidable, a part of the drama and the price of living in a free society with open access to the courts. Hurray for that, but the bedrock of the system is that the courts will try to be fair, even if sometimes wildly inconsistent.

Texas, like America, is a politically divided society, split almost equally between more liberal Democrats and more conservative Republicans. Many people surmise that Democrats are more open to the claims of the injured, such as the victims of exposure to asbestos. You won't find anything in this book to contradict that. After all, in most states with Republican-voting majorities, asbestos litigation has been effectively terminated by legislative limits on recovery. The same theory about politics intruding on the courts is true in cases of medical malpractice injury. How about alleged economic fraud? Is the entire state of Texas inhospitable to large damages for business fraud? Politics intrude again. While Texas is the most-Republican large state in the union, some of its largest metropolitan areas are not.

The voters of Dallas County elect all the judges of the Dallas County trial courts. At the moment, all of the trial judges are Democrats because Dallas County itself, in strong contrast to its suburban neighbors, is dominantly Democratic. And those Democratic judges often reflect in their rulings a leaning toward compensation of victims, as portrayed by their lawyers. All is not lost. The court of appeals, to which any Dallas County case can be appealed, is Republican because those judges are elected from a multicounty electorate. However, even Republican-dominated courts can be grossly unfair in cases involving the politically well-connected, especially in cases involving the law firms who finance their campaigns. Houston, the largest city in Texas, is similar. Houston also enjoys the honor of having hosted much of the legal fabrication known as *Pennzoil v. Texaco*, the greatest white-collar crime of all time.

The lesson to be taken to heart is wariness. Elected judges, and there is much to be said in favor of that system, sometimes play favorites. Unlimited faith in the fairness of the judicial process in Texas or elsewhere is unwarranted.

Guarantees of indebtedness are not covered completely in this chapter. I am just touching on this subject at this point because it is covered in a later chapter. Be very sure that you understand the significance of your personal guarantee of someone else's conduct. In almost all business circumstances, when you sign a personal guarantee as to a bank of the indebtedness of a business, you are personally liable for all, and I mean all, losses which include the original debt, any further advances, all interest, all penalty interest, and all costs of collection.

All of the risk involved in a personal guarantee can take the amount you owe to a staggering figure. Take no comfort in the fact that others may also have guaranteed the debt. The holder of the guarantee will direct his efforts at whomever he believes can be made to pay first. You may have resulting rights against the other guarantors—that's called contribution—but it is likely to be useless. If you take away from this book only one thought, I hope it is the traditional lawyer's wisdom that the best definition of a guarantor is "a schmuck with a fountain pen." A final caution on this topic—all sorts of common agreements for services rendered to a business corporation, such as telephone, travel, limousines, and the like contain a second signature line for your personal signature that commits you to your personal guarantee of the contract. Never, never sign that line! Mark through it!

Last is the issue of medical bills that result from a very murky and dangerous environment; this includes the world of huge medical expense and the resulting liabilities for payment. It is very difficult to criticize by name the great medical institutions of America—the Mayo Clinic in Rochester, Minnesota; the Cleveland Clinic; MD Anderson in Houston; and the like. Their innovations in medicine have saved countless lives. Their doctors and staff are the best in the world. The care afforded has no parallel, and the environment is as helping and friendly to very ill patients as anyone can imagine.

The respect, and in many personal cases, the gratitude that many medical institutions fully earned is immense. But those wonderfully trained and sympathetic individuals do not write the rules for or participate in the economic activity of the medical centers, particularly in billing and collecting from patients and all others, not necessarily just close family, who, at the moment of greatest need, agreed to be personally responsible for all medical care and expenses. The glaring, flagrant injustices of medical collection, particularly by large hospitals and their affiliates, are just beginning to see the light of day. In his cover story for *Time Magazine* dated February 20, 2013, Steven Brill, an investigative reporter, wrote an entirely chilling, almost nauseating exposé of hospital charges divided into three categories: reasonable, too high, and essentially criminal.

Brill covered in detail the extraction or extortion of $83,900 from a middle-class family for initial doses of chemotherapy for non-Hodgkin's lymphoma for a family member. Each adult family member signed a personal guarantee without any limit or even an idea of what the charges would be. Brill's discussion dissected the essential fraud in the system—insurance companies pay exponentially less for the same medical applications as do the uninsured or underinsured, who pay 200–300 percent more than well-insured, at least. Charges for all tangible medicinal devices are grossly inflated. The celebrated Yale-New Haven Hospital charged an individual $6,538 for three CT scans, which revealed a broken nose that required no further treatment. Medicare by its contract would have paid $825 for all three scans.

Other horror stories abound. A medical patient from Fort Worth suffering from acute diabetes entered one of the great medical facilities in America. He and his family were not alerted to the termination of Medicare benefits as his hospital stay continued. The final bill was just under $2 million. It was paid, leaving the family destitute.

This more-recent, much-smaller instance showed up in the local newspaper. The family agreed to be responsible for medical care outside of Medicare. Their loved one, an eighty-seven-year-old woman, recovered from visible disease and was transferred to a local hospital for observation. Nothing observed required further treatment. The bill for three days of observation exceeded $30,000. Medicare does not pay for observation. No one told them. And, finally, on May 8, 2013, the *New York Times* reported on the huge variances in hospital costs for the same courses of treatment. The dice are loaded against those financially responsible for care.

Be careful. Do not get elected as the only hero of the moment. Do not guarantee the hospital bill—no matter what screams of anguish at your lack of love, sympathy, and friendship. Contribute cash as a deposit against the bill. Get a written estimate with a binding cap on your exposure. Negotiate on whatever insurance is available. If necessary, make it clear that you will dictate a change to a different hospital to get a more reasonable price. Read the Brill article and beware. If you guarantee the full course of treatment, you may easily be looking at $250,000 or more. Do not do that.

Think each of these scenarios through. If you don't need a formal asset-protection plan (APP), don't buy one—for sure, don't buy a prepackaged plan. If you think you might rest easier with an APP, visit a lawyer in your state who works in the arena. You'll come to a proper decision.

— 4 —

Texas Two-Stepping on Your Own Toes: Can You Create Your Personal APP?

Can you create an adequate APP for yourself? The odds are against it. First, it is important to explore what adequate asset protection consists of in a mechanical and functional sense. Every lawyer who practices in this area has experienced the client with the *Magic Plan*. The client recites with some pride that he has spent $22,000 on the very best of all asset protection plans, and he just needs an hour of the lawyer's time to glance through the documents and approve them. The documents are then fetched and put on the table: a lovely, forty-six page family limited partnership. This plan can be acquired in its standard form on the Internet. It isn't worth much. In this case, the magic plan is often too long and too expensive, and it's hard to tell a friend that the famous New York attorney did not forget anything important—except one thing—actually putting the family assets into the family limited partnership. Sadly this happens all too often. The careful protection of many assets involves technical knowledge.

The best known and saddest incident of this type of misadventure with a family limited partnership involved Michael Jackson, the brilliant but famously strange musician. According to his posthumous records, he paid a huge sum for a long, legally competent family limited partnership, and then he and his attorney failed to put any assets into it. Actually, folks, it's not real hard. A bill of sale will transfer ownership of most personal property such as jewelry, paintings, and stamp and gun collections. Transfers of ownership on securities and investment accounts and deeds to investment real estate and vacation homes are not technically difficult. Nothing hard to do, but Jackson and his advisors never got around to doing it or updating it, as the case may be. The family limited partnership does not protect any asset that is not legally placed within it.

The second important matter to consider for Texas residents is to go down the asset list and determine what property is exempt under Texas law. It's elementary, but you would be surprised at how often the exempted assets are casually placed and titled in an artificial legal entity, thereby changing the legal ownership and forfeiting the statutory exemptions.

If your affairs are complex, you will probably need several limited liability companies—one to manage the family limited partnership, another to manage the management entity itself, and several more, each to conduct defined activities of a similar economic nature. Never make yourself the general partner. That forfeits all of the asset-protection advantages of the family limited partnership.

In order to take full advantage of a sophisticated APP, the several entities need to be coordinated, and their purposes and initial activities documented. That is done in the form of minutes of the initial meeting of the limited partnership and a written declaration of purpose as to the several LLCs. Additional minutes should describe later transactions. While there is no magic formula or even magic words, the assistance of a capable lawyer is important. You may have to explain later in the presence of ill-tempered creditors or their representatives exactly what you did and why you did it. All of that brings into play another bit of time-honored legal wisdom: "Faded ink is better than a good memory."

For most folks, the creation of an APP should never be a do-it-yourself project. You may have considered acquiring a basic set of documents from the Internet, or even from a friend who paid for them, and then doing all the title transfers yourself. Although personal property is often transferred by a common bill of sale, it still has to be done right. Real estate can be transferred only by written conveyance—usually a deed. Some skill in conveyance is required. Sometimes it is difficult to get the deed recorded. Deed recordings must be properly acknowledged by a notary. Some jurisdictions have very particular requirements. For example, in Hood County, Texas, not far from Fort Worth, a deed may not be recorded without the foregoing legend in a required typeset:

NOTICE OF CONFIDENTIALTY RIGHTS: IF YOU ARE A NATURAL PERSON, YOU MAY REMOVE OR STRIKE ANY OR ALL OF THE FOLLOWING INFORMATION FROM ANY INSTRUMENT THAT TRANSFERS AN INTEREST IN REAL PROPERTY BEFORE IT IS FILED FOR RECORD IN THE PUBLIC RECORDS: SOCIAL SECURITY NUMBER OR YOUR DRIVER'S LICENSE NUMBER.

I don't know why Hood County requires this language. When asked, the county clerk did not know either. Corporate securities must be transferred by assignment with Medallion Guarantees and also electronically. There are assets that require specialized conveyances such as vehicles, boats, and aircraft. Please visit a lawyer. Don't try to do it yourself. Small errors may have bad consequences.

Everything's Bigger in Texas:
Generational Versus
Self-Settled Trusts

All of us are reluctant to deliberately, and somewhat
expensively, re-order our lives—particularly our
financial lives. Even though we realize that we may be
a target defendant, someone with money whom a lawyer will be thrilled to sue, there isn't an easy or simple
method to achieve financial peace of mind. After all,
the events we are protecting ourselves against will probably not happen. What about employing a trust to hold
your assets?

Historically there has been a connection in the inter-
play between creditors and certain debtors who are the
beneficiaries of trusts. Most of us have heard the term,
often spoken derisively, "trust baby." This conveys the
image of a seemingly rich, self-indulgent playboy who
has been fortunate in his choice of ancestors. Someone
who had amassed a fortune placed significant values in
a trust that benefits an heir. His creditors found they

could not invade the trust. By long practice, most such trusts were specifically designed as a "spendthrift" trust, which means that the playboy beneficiary has no legal power to touch the corpus of the trust or to assign away his future income. He was free to spend what he received—nothing more—but it was often plenty, and his creditors had no right to it.

Note the essential design of such arrangements. The grantors or the folks who earned the money, known technically as the corpus of the trust, placed these assets in a formal, written trust, thus creating financial benefits for a descendant or a group of descendants. Thus, a generational trust was created. The designated trustee was empowered and directed to distribute financial benefits as long as he had the money to the beneficiaries, usually descendants of the grantors. There are many differing distribution schemes, but the most common are distributions to provide for the health, education, maintenance, and support of the beneficiary or beneficiaries. These so-called HEMS trusts are not tied to any published monetary minimum or maximum scale of distributions. Assuming the resources are sufficient, the amount and timing of the distribution is left to the reasonable discretion of the trustee. Prior to 1968, the truly rich could establish a generation-skipping trust (GST), by the terms of which a family fortune could descend for a very long time without being taxed by the IRS. In trusts without the GST feature, the government asserts that the decedent owned for tax purposes a part of the values in the trust, and accordingly, estate tax arises upon his death. That is a pure tax concept and hard to understand, but it stops the transfer of wealth from passing down a family tree untaxed.

You can't do that anymore because GSTs were prohibited, insofar as the nontaxability of trust value in the estate of a beneficiary in 1968. But it was fun while it lasted, and a surprising number of grand, entrusted fortunes still retain the generation-skipping benefits available by creation prior to 1968. That's because good draftsmen extended the generation-skipping trust benefits until the death of the last named beneficiary who was alive when the trust was created. It's only been forty-six years or so, people can live a long time, and for some, but not all, a lot of money delivered monthly makes a very long life quite pleasurable.

You have likely already noticed the significant difference between these trust beneficiaries and you. They had generous ancestors who amassed great fortunes and were kind to their descendants. You and I, unfortunately, did not. So the question raised is whether a trust format effectively serves the purpose of asset protection, defined as protection against your creditors, when it's all your money. On the balance, there are two answers: maybe and no. The maybe answer applies when you create and fund your asset-protection trust before you have encountered a potential or existing large hostile creditor, and while you, by any reasonable test, are solvent. Under those circumstances, in those happy times, the trust can be serviceable, but it is hard to find the right trustee and successor. There are issues regarding how much control over the assets you can retain; the distributions are taxable and the tax accounting can be expensive. A trust created by you for you may have some advantages, but the effective use of family limited partnerships and the single-entity limited liability company for each separate economic activity is more flexible, cheaper to administer, and just better.

The information I've given you so far is the good news about trusts. If you already have suffered large losses, or it's likely you will, trusts do little good. And if you fall for one or more of the gimmick trusts, those that promise forever protection against known or likely creditors, you have made a huge mistake. To appreciate the problem, you must understand the self-settled trust.

The self-settled trust is precisely what its name implies. An individual or married couple places their assets in a legally competent trust with the understanding that the trustee of the trust will refuse to turn those assets over to the grantor's creditors, even if they hold final judgments against the grantors. In Texas, there is simply no debate. Under Texas law, a self-settled trust is valid, not illusionary or fraudulent, but none of its assets are in any way protected from creditor claims. Texas courts simply treat those trust assets as your money.

In the early 1990s, a new fad arose, the foreign-asset protection trust. That concept was faulty for several reasons, and the fad has proved faulty. Why was establishing your trust in a foreign—often very obscure—jurisdiction a defective plan? First, and never to be underestimated, is that it just looks bad. Displaying to your creditors your foreign trust causes them to think you are a crook. And, speaking of crooks, your faraway trustee might also be a crook and cheat you. More importantly, a judge reviewing these circumstances will not believe that you, the debtor, do not have control of the assets.

With the recognized failure of most foreign trusts to provide asset protection, several states moved into the space. By state statute, the authorized self-settled asset-protection trust came into fashion. These are termed domestic asset-protection trusts (DAPT). Some fifteen states passed laws welcoming DAPTs in their jurisdictions. The concept of attracting a lot of money to a particular state is welcomed by the state's banks and, hence, attractive to local politicians. They vary some, but it is fair to use the Alaska statute as the role model. Unfortunately a bit of technical explanation is necessary.

To achieve the benefits embodied in the statute of a welcoming state, you don't have to be a resident of that state. In Alaska, for example, you must submit a trust document that contains certain essential provisions:

» The trust must be irrevocable.

» The trust instrument must expressly state that the trust adopts Alaskan law as pertains to validity, construction, and administration.

» The trust instrument must contain spendthrift provisions.

» At least some assets should be in Alaska, under the control of an Alaskan trustee—this is not mandatory, but the placement seems to add to legitimacy.

There are others. Alaska has amended its statute ten times. Does it really work? Can your creditors pierce it? On balance, unfortunately, they can.

The most important case involved Mr. T. W. Mortensen who formed the Mortensen Seldovia Trust "to maximize the protection of the trust estate . . . from creditors' claims . . . and to minimize all wealth transfer taxes." Mr. Mortensen affirmed, as Alaska law required, that he was solvent at the time of entrustment and did not intend to defraud his creditors. That statement was found to be untrue by the bankruptcy judge in Alaska, even though there was no one specific, large, unpaid creditor. So, as you have guessed, the bankruptcy judge said "Nothing doing."

The assets of the Mortensen Seldovia Trust were collapsed and made available to Mr. Mortensen's creditors. All of the reasoning is not important; the result is that a self-settled trust is vulnerable to creditors. The court went to some pains to state that Mortensen's declaration that he did not intend to beat his creditors was not in and of itself totally condemning, but that's what most of us think the decision means.

Several other states passed statutes promoting themselves as a great venue for your self-settled trust. None of those statutes is any better than the Alaskan law. In addition to Alaska, Colorado, Delaware, Hawaii, and Missouri passed similar laws. Other states that have something akin to the Alaskan law are Nevada, New Hampshire, Oklahoma, and Rhode Island. You need to think long and hard about the legalities of whatever asset-protection plan you decide to use, inside or outside of your state of residence. If you choose a trust, it must be capable of protecting you in good times and not-so-good times. The lesson is that a DAPT is not a magic cloak.

All Hat, No Cattle:
Asset Protection via the Internet

Asset protection is promoted all over the Internet in the form of pop-ups, automatic references, and teaser ads that promise total protection from all creditors. If you chose to read this book, you are way too smart to believe in a magic or a one-size-fits-all approach to this subject. Nonetheless, some of the advertisements and enticements are interesting because they shed light on the problems, even if they do not reach a formulated plan.

The following generally valid statements are collated from a dozen or more sales pitches:

» Construct and implement your APP plan as early in your financial life as possible. The more years the ink is dry before the financial crisis intrudes, the better for you.

» Use your state exemptions. If you live in Texas really, really use your state exemptions.

» The essence of asset protection is divestment of personal title to valuable assets. Ah, but where to put them?

At this point, the sales pitches diverge, and many are based on the deficiencies in the concepts recommended by others. It's negative salesmanship, but it is worthy of consideration.

Disregarding the pure scams and frauds that I think you will recognize, most of the focus of Internet promotions is on various iterations of the self-settled trust. This trust is established by an individual who places his own assets into a trust for his own benefit and, at least on the face of the documents, turns over to a trustee much, if not all, of the power and responsibility to manage these assets. Because the assets are legally titled to and under the legal control of someone else, they cannot be seized by a creditor of the entrustor, i.e., the creator of the trust.

Debtors and potential debtors have long been fascinated by the possible utility of an irrevocable trust. The implication of the word "irrevocable" is easy to understand: the trust cannot be materially changed by its creator to benefit the creator. In the usual case, the grantor or the creator creates the trust, declares it to be irrevocable, and legally delivers to the designated trustee cash and other assets, sometimes including real estate. The trustee is empowered to make distributions to the grantor's spouse and children but barred from making any distributions to the grantor. In a state like Texas that follows the community property doctrine—distributions to the spouse require special care.

State-of-the-art irrevocable trusts allow the grantor to retain and exercise a special power of appointment. By the use of such power, the grantor may remove and replace the trustee and may in the event of estrangement or divorce remove his or her spouse from the roster of permitted recipients of distribution from the trust. All is well so long as the grantor does nothing that attempts to violate the exclusion of the grantor himself from the roster of permitted beneficiaries.

At first blush, it appears that one of the most important rules has been satisfied—legal title to the assets has been placed in the name of someone else. And sometimes the second hurdle has also been jumped—the ink was dry on both the trust and the legal transfers of assets before the sad events occurred that resulted in large liabilities owed by the trust founder. How foolproof is this plan?

Of course, and as the detractors of trusts used for asset protection always point out, any asset-protection trust, foreign or domestic, whether organized under the law of a DAPT state or under a foreign law, is vulnerable to a claim of pre-existing creditor. A pre-existing creditor is someone whose claims arose before the trust process was legally complete and effective.

Put yourself in the shoes of a creditor who has at considerable expense obtained a $3-million judgment against someone. You, the creditor in this example, are angry—you want your money. Are you likely to believe that the individual who wronged you has voluntarily turned his pockets inside out and given all his assets to a trustee in a strange, foreign locality? You would not believe that. Rather you would believe that the trust is a fraud and that the entrustor, the person whose assets are now allegedly maintained in sacred trust, really controls them. Is that true? In about 99 percent of cases, through one mechanism or another, this is true. No one, except perhaps one driven by religious zeal or strange drugs, would deliver significant assets to someone he has never met and divest himself entirely from control.

As a perceptive judge once remarked in a famous case, after announcing his profound disbelief that the entrustor, who owed millions, had delivered millions to a stranger in the Cook Islands and retained no control, "Mr. Wilson, you are just not that kind of guy!"

The judicial doctrine of a deep conviction of disbelief, sometimes called just plain common sense, is the torpedo that sinks most self-settled protective trusts. And worse, a new provision of the Bankruptcy Code, Section 522(o) provides a ten-year look back at all nonexempt property improperly converted to exempt property except for Florida's or Texas's allowable homestead. In those states, making the scheduled, monthly mortgage payments to a legitimate third-party lender is permitted.

Is it best to forget about using any trust as a useful part of an APP? No, not so fast. Legal creativity is not always in vain. Assume again that the trust was created and funded before the storm clouds first appeared. And then consider a very clever concept from a very good lawyer who you can find on the Internet under "541 Trust." He describes a trust technically competent and specifically drafted to satisfy all of the potential requirements that will prevent a trustee in bankruptcy from administering the subject assets for the benefit of the settler's creditors. The material provision of the Bankruptcy Code reads: "11 U.S.C. § 541 (b) Property of the estate does not include (1) any power that the debtor may exercise solely for the benefit of an entity other than the debtor."

Sounds good, and it means what it says. If a debtor has no power to benefit himself, the Section 541 trust prevents a bankruptcy trustee from administering based on the power the trustee normally has to adjudicate who and in what proportion shall benefit from the values in the trust. Once again, there is an important drawback. The 541 trust mechanism does not protect the actual property that the debtor contributed if that donation is proved to have been a fraudulent transfer. That's the law in Texas and pretty much everywhere else where the debt came before the transfers to the trust.

In this arena, a more than casual overview is required. The 541 trust, like other self-settled trusts, is effective but not foolproof and if created late in the day, is subject to the same "conviction of disbelief" that has been the reaction of many judges to such elaborate plans. But suppose it was funded long before any unpaid creditor existed. Stripped to its essence under those conditions, the operative rules are pretty easy to understand: a donor who has no unsatisfied creditors and no reason to identify any prospective creditors may donate property to a self-settled 541 trust.

If such a donor excludes himself or herself from the category of any person who may later benefit by trust distributions, those distributions when made are not subject to claims of the donor's creditors. Additionally, the reservation by the donor of certain special powers of appointment does not invalidate the protection. This means that the right to choose who and in what amounts may from time to time be benefitted is not an asset of the donor reachable by his creditors or, indirectly, by a trustee in bankruptcy. It's complicated and expensive, but it should be judged legally sufficient if every "i" is dotted.

Working out how to structure a trust is hard to step up and do. A lot of planning and a lot of discipline are required. If you stumble and don't get it done, by which I mean planned, fully executed, and funded long before any large claims materialize, many bad things can happen.

The Internet is a wonderful diversion from which you can get interesting ideas and provocative thoughts but do not pay your money and rely on prepackaged, standardized form documents. They will not hold up under legal attack. The ultimate choice may be either to bring your assets back to the US or stay in jail. Neither result is very pleasant.

Lawyers are active on the Internet and elsewhere promoting themselves and their publications and services. That's America. Many are skilled. Some, judged by the nature of their boasts and promises, are not. I offer a suggestion about engaging a new lawyer as asset-protection counsel. Meet the lawyer first. If he or she promises an absolute bar to the enforcement of creditors' rights against you, say good-bye. It isn't possible. If, however, you like the lawyer, and he or she is located in the state where you live, hire that person or someone else like him or her. There are great benefits in so doing.

A practical overview—self-settled trusts can be very useful if done well in advance of storm clouds, and if they are, in all things, technically correct. There are many fine lawyers, including some who advertise heavily on the Internet, who can prepare very well-crafted documents. But frequently it's too late in the game between debtors and creditors for any self-settled trust to provide much benefit.

The laws in the area of self-settled trusts are fairly similar in each state. In a case very interesting to lawyers in this field, the Ninth Federal Circuit denied all claims of a bankruptcy trustee against a trust beneficiary, but the way the court ruled provides little comfort regarding family trusts. Two of the three judges ruled against a California bankruptcy trustee because the settlors of the trust, the challenged beneficiary, and, most importantly, all of the assets were located in Hawaii. Hawaiian law is very favorable to Hawaiian residents. If you are a third-generation Hawaiian and all the contested assets are land in Hawaii, that is great! If not, forget about it.

Even so, the third judge didn't like it. He quoted a whole series of cases saying that, in his opinion, the rights of the creditors were paramount, and that this trust was no shield in California, where the beneficiary had filed bankruptcy.

That is enough legal musing. All self-settled trusts that deny creditors their right to be repaid from the entrusted assets will be attacked. The results will depend on factual circumstances and the mind-set of the judge. So is there any trust but a generational trust that is free from possible attack? I would have said no but for one previous professional experience.

Frankly I never thought much of trusts as asset-protection devices until I met Bill and Phil, twin brothers, who made an appointment and arrived at my office for legal assistance. They did not make the appointment because they wanted my philosophical thoughts or legal opinions, no matter how profound they might have been. They just wanted a trust document drafted exactly in accordance with their plan. They called it the "Trouble Trust." I drafted it as directed. Here was their concept: one of the brothers had just made $1 million or more in a real estate deal. He wanted to put that money in a trust administered by his twin brother as trustee. The money was to be used, in the discretion of the trustee, solely to pay for legal fees, costs, and funds necessary to settle any legal controversy in which his brother, the settlor of the trust, was a defendant—divorce, claims for personal injury, a criminal charge, or anything, but no money could ever go directly to the brother, and the trustee had unlimited discretion. He might step into a mess and achieve peace for his brother, or he might just sit it out. It's his call.

I prepared a rather simple document as the brothers directed. They liked it, signed it, paid for it, and I have not seen either one since. I do have the impression that both have been successful, based on some real estate news I read, but beyond that, I know nothing. But, and this may be important to someone, I strongly believe their Trouble Trust, if effected before the beneficiary has unpaid creditors, is a very sound device. No legal opinion is offered, but if you have a twin you would trust with your financial life and a spare million dollars, give it some thought.

Most of the time, it is better to organize your affairs to limit your ultimate personal risk by adopting and maintaining a consistent practice of employing family limited partnership(s) and limited liability companies. You don't personally own those assets. It is very hard, in Texas as in many other states, for your creditors to reach them and that's where the leverage is. However, there is one more important question to be answered: What's in it for me? Roughly translated, that means how do I get as much money as I want from these complicated artificial enterprises?

That is a good question. There is a simple answer and then a little more complicated answer. The simple answer is that you are the designated manager and entitled to a reasonable salary, which is also free from creditor attack in Texas so long as it is "reasonable." What is reasonable? The answer depends on the value of the assets under management, but $20,000–$25,000 per month is fine if the gross assets require some management and produce the cash flow. Beyond doing that, you can pay yourself more by acquiring or already possessing expertise. If you love to travel, become a travel agent; if you manage the securities portfolio, get some credentials as an investment manager; if you love to trade expensive cars, get some kind of a dealer's license, and so on. In the day of the Internet, degrees and credentials are available to anyone at some price. I would not, however, suggest enrolling in Trump University.

~ 7 ~

Follow Your Head, Not Your Heart: Lenders Are Very Smart

I have represented many persons who found themselves buried under individual, personal indebtedness. There are certain identifiable contributing factors that recur in the majority of instances. If you can faithfully promise that you, your spouse, or your dependent children will never again drive after imbibing any alcohol or drugs, you will escape a common predicament. If you shall never become fully responsible to a financial institution for the obligations of any enterprise or another person beside yourself, you will benefit enormously. After these two goals are achieved, if you can manage to stay out of intensive and vicious personal litigation, you can pretty well stop reading and go to a good movie.

Notice that I did not include personal obligations, knowingly contracted, for personal uses, college, purchased automobiles, the loan on the home you live in and, in most cases, not even loans to establish your business. Most people keep good mental arithmetic on what they know they owe. That includes the debts of their business, although, obviously, those in medicine and the other professions have malpractice risks. Even those, however, can be insured. Unfortunately the problem arises from the unforeseen, unexpected, huge claim that buries folks under a mountain of debt and puts a lifetime of success in jeopardy. DWI, driving while intoxicated, or DUI, driving under the influence, is a big contributor. It doesn't take much alcohol to blow over .08 percent, which is the Texas standard. Your automobile insurance coverage may be more limited than the nice agent explained, and there you are.

Signing an unlimited guarantee is often how people become exposed to unanticipated, large, unmanageable debt(s). Repetition is not a sin. I have proclaimed throughout this effort: don't sign an unlimited guarantee of any part of the financial affairs of others. If I thought it would help, I would spread those words on the bottoms of every open two pages.

Bankers are not fools. They are not without influence in state legislatures. They write the laws about credit. The provisions below are from an unlimited guarantee document on a loan between a major bank, which we shall refer to as "bank," and a "guarantor," a doctor who had unwisely agreed to guarantee the debts of a "borrower."

The guarantor agreed to pay all the debts of the borrower. The bank defined the indebtedness in this way:

Indebtedness means any and all of borrower's liabilities, obligations, debts, and indebtedness to lender, now existing or hereinafter incurred or created, together with all other liabilities, costs, and expenses for which borrower is responsible under the loan agreement, under any loan documents, including, without limitation, the obligations evidenced by the notes, and all other loans, advances, interest, costs, attorneys' fees, debts, overdraft indebtedness, credit card indebtedness, lease obligations, other obligations, and liabilities of borrower, any present or future judgments against borrower, and all renewals, extensions, modifications, substitutions, and rearrangements of the foregoing; and whether any such indebtedness is voluntarily or involuntarily incurred, due or not due, absolute or contingent, direct or indirect, liquidated or un-liquidated, determined or undetermined; whether borrower may be liable individually or jointly with others, or primarily or secondarily, or as debtor, maker, co-maker, drawer, endorser, guarantor, or surety; whether such Indebtedness arises by note, draft acceptance, guarantee, endorsement, letter of credit, assignment, overdraft, indemnity agreement, or otherwise; whether recovery on the indebtedness may be or may become barred or unenforceable against borrower for any reason whatsoever; and whether the Indebtedness arises from the transaction which may be voidable on account of infancy, insanity, ultra vires, or otherwise.

According to the definition above, the guarantor is immediately liable for anything the bank might now or later lend to this dude. That interpretation is backed up by the terms below.

Authorization to Lender

This is the death warrant. "The Guarantor authorizes the Bank to make additional loans to the Borrower, for any reason, in any amount." The guarantor is liable up to any amount. You don't know anyone that well. It is insane to sign such a document. The problem, of course, is that most guarantors do not read the document, nor would they understand it fully if they did. If anyone ever understood the document fully, he or she wouldn't sign it. But logic is not the light of the law.

Nature of Guarantee

The guarantor guarantees payment, not collection. The bank has no duty to look to anyone but the guarantor; even if the borrower and the president of the bank make an unfortunate speculation on the price of gold, no problem. The guarantor is fully liable. There are no offsets for improper conduct by the bank or its officers.

Waiver of Defenses

"Guarantor waives all rights of guarantor under, or the requirements imposed by, Chapter 34 of the Texas Business and Commerce Code. Guarantor also waives any and all rights or defenses arising by reason of (i) any election of remedies by lender which destroys or otherwise adversely affects guarantor's subrogation rights or guarantor's rights to proceed against borrower for reimbursement, including without limitation, any loss of rights guarantor may suffer by reason of any law limiting, qualifying, or discharging the Indebtedness; (ii) any disability or other defense of borrower, of any other guarantor, or of any other person, or by reason of the cessation of borrower's liability from any cause whatsoever, other than payment in full in legal tender of the Indebtedness; (iii) any right to claim discharge of the indebtedness on the basis of unjustified impairment of any collateral for the indebtedness; or (iv) any defenses given to guarantors at law or in equity other than actual payment and performance of indebtedness. This guarantee shall continue to be effective or be reinstated, as the case may be, if at any time any payment of all or any part of the indebtedness is rescinded or must otherwise be returned by lender upon the insolvency, bankruptcy, or reorganization of borrower, guarantor, any other guarantor of all or any part of the indebtedness, or otherwise, all as though such payment had not been made."

If you never previously paid close attention to standard forms handed to you by banks, credit card companies, and others to whom you will owe money, please be very cautious in the future. There is an infinite variety of other, less-extreme forms standing behind each other in a financial transaction. The single most effective is absolutely to limit your exposure by a provision stating you shall never be liable for more than say $50,000. But do not act as your own lawyer. The bank and its many lawyers, with their experience in these matters, are smarter than you.

Debts, once contracted, are not always processed the same way by creditors. Fifty years ago, a hard-nosed debt collector in Fort Worth known as Texas Consumer Finance parked a bright-yellow panel truck in front of the homes of folks who owed it money; rang a big, loud bell; and told all who inquired that the residents of the affected house were considered "deadbeats." It was effective until it was stopped by a court and, later, by a statute. These were, to be sure, relatively small debts, maybe $3,500 maximum. Nonetheless there was pain and shame in being publically called out loudly and locally as a defaulting debtor.

Everyone recognizes that a balance must be struck between the legitimate right of a creditor to collect the debt owed to him and the rights, more inferred than constitutional, of persons to not have their lives ruined by aggressive debt collection. But what's the balance?

And who decides? Where does this struggle come from? And where is it going?

Many scholarly articles have been written about the tension between debtors and creditors. For example, Professor Lea Shepard in "Creditors' Contempt" (*Brigham Young University Law Review*, Vol. 1509) relates that an unsecured judgment creditor, one with no lien, mortgage, or security interest on the property of the debtor, has two basic ways to attempt to satisfy its judgment. It may bring an *in rem* action directed against specific property owned or believed owned by the debtor or it may pursue an *in personam* remedy that means the debtor will sue you individually. The intrinsic problem with *in rem* actions is that the creditor may not know where to look and, even more likely, if the creditor locates real or personal property, someone else probably has an earlier, perfected mortgage, lien, or security interest encumbering the property discovered.

What happens when the creditor precedes *in personam* by legal process to require the debtor personally to do things? Depositions are solicited. Interrogatories, questions to be answered under oath, are delivered—the legal term is "propounded." The creditor may run garnishments, an effort to collect money from your bank account, and, in many jurisdictions, a creditor may file an equitable action to require his debtor to turn over assets to satisfy debts. If the debtor refuses to comply with the orders of a court, issued at the behest of his creditor, he may be charged with contempt of court, which may be enforced by imprisonment. Then the classic constitutional issue is reached. If a debtor cannot be imprisoned for debt, and almost every state constitution so provides, how can it be constitutional to imprison him for failure to cooperate in the process of debt collection? The courts have very mixed records. Some say debt collection is debt collection, and no part of that process, except proven perjury, should lead to prison. Others, probably most, have said that failure by a debtor to appear or to furnish requested information, referred to as "non-appearance contempt" can lead to prison.

Back and forth the legal struggles go. Truly egregious conduct by creditors elicits sympathy and support for debtors, particularly those who really do not appear to have much, while a debtor's apparent contempt for the entire legal process makes the court mad. There really is no final answer to these confrontations, except, sometimes, bankruptcy. It is safe, however, to conclude that being the besieged debtor is absolutely no fun whether you owe $3,500 you can't pay or $35 million. Do not take that risk. A proper asset-protection plan, at least for those with meaningful assets, is far, far better.

While it is true that there are certain debts that no one likes to pay, such as alimony, federal income taxes, and the judgment your former partner obtained against you from that lay-down jury and incompetent judge. But the fact that one doesn't want to pay a debt is not a legal reason not to pay it. However those who don't want to pay really don't want to pay, even if they can pay, and comprise the market for a lot of debt-avoidance ideas ranging from crackpot to criminal.

To those who deny the right or authority of our federal government to tax their income or to collect back taxes from liquidation of their assets, a claimed defense is the common law trust, also billed as the constitutional common law trust. The theory is that if you separate yourself from direct receipt of salary and other compensation, then a reasonable interpretation of the laws of the United States would be that your self-settled trust, allegedly located in a jurisdiction outside the United States, would not owe the income tax on what it might give you or provide for you. Balderdash, an old-fashioned term, applies to this theory. If you, in fact, earn the income, then you, in fact, owe the income tax. If you desire to discuss this further, you might communicate with the once-very-successful movie actor Wesley Snipes, who spent three years in a federal prison for tax evasion. Mr. Snipes did not believe he owed income tax; the federal government thought otherwise. The government won.

Other popular schemes include the false generation of huge interest expense by means of phony second mortgages on your property. The "of record" second mortgagee is, of course, a foreign entity. But when real money did not change hands, there was no true mortgage, and there is still plenty of room in federal prisons for those who choose this scam.

Others have, unfortunately, placed faith in entities such as a Cook Islands trust, Nevis limited liability companies, trusts organized under the laws of the Isle of Man, and other exotic locales. It is not so much that all of these devices are intrinsically worthless; it is simply that you will do better by giving careful consideration of your interests under the laws of your state.

Don't put your assets in any of those exotic offshore entities. If they sound too good to be true, they are not true. They don't work, and the penalties are trying and severe.

Quality asset protection depends upon your putting the necessary transfers and restrictions on transfers in place before you become liable for more than you can pay. Once a huge liability is established, and, sometimes, before it is finally established but after it appears likely, the assets you deal with may later be subject to creditor attack as fraudulent transfers. If it is legally determined to be a fraudulent transfer, all sorts of bad things may follow:

- » The transfer(s) may be set aside or unwound.
- » Your friends or family members may be sued for the value of what was transferred or more.
- » You may have exposed yourself to the now, very unfriendly bankruptcy provisions in Sec. 522(o)

of the Bankruptcy Code, which may cost you the benefit of exemptions to which you would otherwise be entitled. The look back period under § 522(o) is an astonishing ten years.

Do not take this risk. Put your basic asset-protection plan (APP) into operational status while you are solvent. Being solvent means the fair value of your assets exceeds your liabilities, including contingent liabilities like the lawsuit pending against you that you believe to be without merit.

The judgment of your creditors on the critical issue of whether you were solvent or insolvent when you designed your APP will not be as kind to you as yours. Acquire the basic APP before the adverse events. If one occurs, acquire the APP as soon as possible and deal, however unhappily, with the early creditor.

Construct and acquire a competent APP with the counsel of competent practitioners, not from an Internet-promoted fantasy or fraud. In this case, the better plan is not just better—it is cheaper. Obviously major financial setbacks with major exposure can arise from unlimited causes. It is impossible to avoid all risk, regardless of how much exercise of care and caution you use. You are the best judge of the risk facts inherent in your lifestyle. After reading this chapter, weigh them, and if the scales tilt, act on that information.

✥ 8 ✥

Drawing a Line in the Sand: More on the Rights of a Creditor in Texas

The field of battle between creditors and debtors who owe them money in Texas, as in several other states, has a split personality. Creditors, particularly banks and other lenders, own the currently highly Republican Texas Legislature. No one but a Republican has been elected to a statewide office in over fifteen years. However, the Texas tradition of affording debtors who play by the rules the opportunity to safeguard important parts of their personal holdings is very deeply rooted.

On the balance, an individual who has protected his family by the procedures described in this book has an excellent chance of financial recovery, but one who has not will be harshly treated. It is in your best interest to review now the legal weapons of a creditor. A creditor is someone who is properly and lawfully owed money by another. A creditor fighting for a judgment against someone is still a creditor, but we are focused on the creditor who today holds a final judgment against a person.

A judgment creditor will seek satisfaction of his judgment by levying, sometimes called executing, on the debtor's nonexempt assets. That process as to non-real property involves a sheriff or constable who tags the subject property and goes on to hold an advertised sale with the proceeds, net of costs to be applied against the debt. This is not a much-advertised sale; bidders are normally few, particularly because the judgment creditor can bid by credit against his debt; that is, up to the full amount of the judgment, the creditor may bid without tendering cash. It's a big advantage.

As to real estate, the creditors may file an abstract of his judgment in every county in Texas where he thinks the debtor may own real property. If so, the abstracted judgment becomes an enforceable lien on the real property of the debtor, subject only to prior legally enforceable liens.

Suppose the debtor has transferred his property, both real and personal, to his close friends and relatives. Texas adopted the Uniform Fraudulent Transfer Act in 1987. An "improper" transfer, meaning one made with actual intent to hinder, delay, or defraud creditors may be set aside, and the creditor may then levy on the proceeds or on the proceeds of the prior sale, if you can find them. And to show that the legislature was serious, a transfer, not actually fraudulent, can be found by a court to be constructively fraudulent if the price paid was too low and the debtor was insolvent or well down the road to insolvency. Creditors have no sense of humor.

A debtor may not convert nonexempt assets into exempt assets to defraud his creditors. If he does and gets caught, the newly acquired "exempt" property may lose all or a part of its exemption but, happily, the debtor may pay off the mortgage on his exempt homestead.

There are also prejudgment procedures, such as writs of attachment, that seek to prevent a likely debtor from secreting or changing the character of his assets. A like procedure, sequestration, seeks to restrain the likely debtor from disposing of a specific asset.

Finally, after a final, nonappealable judgment has been obtained, a creditor may seek appointment of a receiver for all or some of the alleged nonexempt assets of the debtor. Seeking this method of repayment is a burdensome, very-expensive proceeding.

Being a debtor is not fun, particularly in cases in which the creditor is both rich and angry. He may levy writs of garnishment against bank accounts or other financial holdings of his debtor. He may take postjudgment depositions to discover assets he can seize and may seek a turnover of assets or their replacements believed to be subject to levy or seizure. He may require frequent sworn answers to interrogatories that result in harassment and potential heartache.

The outline of our preferred solution to all these vexing problems involves presenting to creditors, as soon as the law compels it, but no sooner, some variation of the following state of the debtor's affairs. There should be a clear, descriptive outline of those assets, real and personal, that the debtor would claim as exempt under Texas law or the law of any other state of residence. Is Texas best? Yes, it is, but many other states have reasonable exemptions as well. The claim of exemption must follow the applicable state law governing such exemptions. Then a debtor may display, by clear evidence, the entities he or she has selected for doing business.

Clear evidence means that the formation and proper administration of a family-limited partnership (FLP) was formed, properly executed, and utilized well before the arrival of the hostile creditor. The FLP owns all sorts of things of value from cash to jewelry to non-homestead real estate to financial assets, all conveyed and assigned properly to the FLP a long time ago. The creditor does not have to take your word for it, nor would he. There are documents in proper form that affected all these transfers, and there are minutes of the annual meeting of the general partner and all other partners in the FLP that detail the nature of all the transfers, and if it was all done before the debt came into view, the FLP itself does not owe a dime.

To complete the presentation, the debtor may explain his use of one or several separate Texas or other state limited liability companies in which he conducts his primary business. As an example, I'll say he was investing in small shopping centers. Each will be owned by a separate limited liability company. Don't despair— it's a cheap form of insurance. There is a separate LLC in which his wife conducts her practice of family counseling and maybe another for a vacation home that is rented.

All economic activities are housed in LLCs. Thus, there are no assets that may be levied on, nothing to sequester, nothing to turn over, nothing to declare in response to a garnishment, nothing upon which to execute because none of these entities is liable to the judgment creditor for anything.

So yes, Mr. Smith does deeply regret drinking too much, driving poorly, and, as the jury found, being responsible for 41 percent of a bad, bad wreck. Thank God no one was killed, but the $4-million judgment that came out of the litigation that became $3 million after application of all insurance will not ruin his life and destroy his family savings. It's a tough world—protecting the values you have earned from a lifetime of hard work is not contrary to God's law. It is both risky and foolish not to do so.

Debts as Vast as Texas: Why Not File Bankruptcy?

Why not, indeed, just file bankruptcy? First, it is important to distinguish between the elective portions of the bankruptcy statute. As an individual debtor, a living, breathing human being, who wants to file for bankruptcy protection, you have four options: Chapter 7, Chapter 11, Chapter 12, or Chapter 13. A business entity, such as a corporation, a partnership, or a limited liability company—not a living, breathing, human being—has two options available: Chapter 7 or Chapter 11. Chapter 12 is reserved for commercial fisherman and family farmers.

Chapter 13 is primarily for consumer debtors. If you owe more than $360,475 in noncontingent, liquated, unsecured debt or more than $1,081,400 in secured debt like a mortgage, you are not eligible for Chapter 13 relief. In Chapter 13, you are required to propose a plan to devote all of your disposable income for five years to repaying your creditors. At the end of five years, if you complete your plan, you would receive a discharge for some or all of your remaining prebankruptcy debts.

If you have signed a guarantee of a real estate loan or a commercial loan that has gone bad, you probably owe too much to file for Chapter 13. In addition, you probably do not want to devote five years to paying off creditors unless you have no other practical choice. Chapter 13 makes sense for a consumer debtor trying to save a house or a car. Occasionally it makes sense for people whose primary debt is delinquent income taxes. The Chapter 13 plan creates a five-year payout period in which the debtor/taxpayer can prioritize tax debt over repayment to other creditors. If you are reading this book, the chances are that Chapter 13 is not an appropriate choice for you.

Chapter 7 is straight liquidation under the direction of a bankruptcy trustee appointed by the United States Trustee's Office, which is part of the United States Department of Justice Civil Division. The trustee will take possession of all nonexempt assets, sell them, collect the money, and make a distribution to creditors. Chapter 7 is equally available to individuals and to business entities.

Chapter 7 has certain advantages. First, the trustee rather than you is responsible for administering the assets in bankruptcy. That shifts the administrative burden to someone else and lets you focus on earning income for the future. Second, an individual debtor will usually receive a discharge of his prebankruptcy debts, except for child support, spousal support, and tax debts, which are usually nondischargeable.

Remember that Uncle Sam writes the laws. He looks out for himself first by collecting taxes off the top. Generally speaking, business debts are dischargeable in bankruptcy, unless you have given creditors false financial information, which you should never do. Third, money you earn after the Chapter 7 case is filed belongs to you, not to the bankruptcy estate. Chapter 7 does not require you to devote any of your future income to the payment of your debts, unlike Chapter 13. The disadvantage of Chapter 7 is that it entails a straight liquidation. While you generally get a discharge of your prebankruptcy debt, you have to surrender all of your nonexempt assets to the trustee.

There are two important things to remember about Chapter 7: 1) Only individuals have exemptions. Business entities have no exemptions and must surrender everything to the trustee. 2) Personal exemptions vary from state to state, being generous in Texas and Florida but harsh in many states, such as Alabama or Pennsylvania. You would have very little left after the Chapter 7, though everything you earn after the case is filed belongs to you, not the Chapter 7 bankruptcy estate. You must consult with a competent bankruptcy lawyer to understand the exemptions that may be available to you in your home state.

Chapter 7 makes sense for three types of individual debtors: those who have no significant assets and just need a discharge to start over; debtors with large amounts of exempt assets in states with generous exemptions, like Texas and Florida; and debtors who still have a lot of future earning potential. If you are a professional baseball player or a neurosurgeon, and you have the ability to earn several million dollars after your bankruptcy through your work or personal services, Chapter 7 may work for you.

Since business entities have no exemptions, they will lose all of their assets in a Chapter 7 case. The trustee will liquidate everything and make a distribution to creditors. A Chapter 7 filing makes sense for a business entity only if its financial condition is beyond healing, and all it needs is a decent burial.

If a business appears salvageable, Chapter 11 is generally the best option. Sometimes corporations and other business entities can recover and prosper given a little time, some relief from creditor demands, and some new financing. Chapter 11 may provide those opportunities. Occasionally a really good idea does not reach the point of profitability before anxious creditors close in, but it may still be a good idea. If an idea really makes sense and someone is willing to put up a little new money, a bankruptcy judge will usually give the enterprise some time to reorganize its affairs and to purpose a plan to pay its creditors.

There are some significant complications with respect to what may constitute a confirmable plan of reorganization, but Chapter 11 provides a fairly clear legal framework for either the rehabilitation or the orderly sale of the business. If the corporation holds valuable or potentially profitable rights and assets, reorganization under Chapter 11 is the preferred course.

Chapter 11 is available to individuals as well. The administrative costs of Chapter 11 are pretty high. Most people cannot afford them, but for those who can, Chapter 11 has potential advantages over Chapter 7. The principal advantage is the ability to keep nonexempt assets that would otherwise be lost in a Chapter 7. This can be significant if those assets are worth far more in the hands of the debtor than they would be in the hands of Chapter 7 trustee, who would simply auction them to the highest bidder or sell them on eBay.

An example of this type of dilemma is a restaurant owner who made a bad investment in a land deal, but who can make far more money from running his restaurant than the Chapter 7 trustee could. For him, a Chapter 11 that left him running his restaurant might be a far better deal for him and his creditors than a Chapter 7. If you have substantial earning potential and nonexempt assets that you want to keep, an individual Chapter 11 case might sense. The disadvantage of an individual Chapter 11 case is the requirement that you devote at least a portion of future income to repaying creditors.

If bankruptcy has all of these wonderful advantages for the financially distressed, why not file? There are several reasons why bankruptcy may not serve your best interests. First and foremost is control. Once you file bankruptcy, someone else makes financial decisions about your life.

In a Chapter 7, the trustee will take all of your non-exempt assets. That means he or she will take your boat, your lake house, and all of your expensive toys. In Texas, you can keep your homestead, your insurance policies, and your IRA or tax-qualified retirement plan, but you will suffer a major downsizing in lifestyle.

In a Chapter 13, you will lose your expensive toys as well, and your financial decisions will be reviewed by the standing Chapter 13 trustee and by the bankruptcy court. You are subject to supervision for five years and will lose five years of disposable income, after basic living expenses, to your creditors.

In a Chapter 11 case, you are in charge, but all of your major decisions will be monitored by your creditors and reviewed by the bankruptcy judge. You have more discretion and control than you would in a Chapter 7 case, but you are not the boss anymore. Any major decisions about your financial affairs must be presented to the bankruptcy judge for his or her approval or disapproval, and you have to devote at least some of your future income to the plan of reorganization.

The second reason bankruptcy may not be the best answer for you is cost. While Chapter 7 is fairly inexpensive, at least with respect to attorneys' fees, all Chapter 11 cases are expensive to administer. Even a relatively small, individual Chapter 11 case may cost hundreds of thousands of dollars in professional fees to attorneys and accountants if the creditors are determined and angry.

The third issue to consider is information. Outside of bankruptcy, you don't have to tell your creditors what you have. They have certain tools to find out through online research and formal post-judgment discovery, such as interrogatories or depositions; however, you don't have to volunteer information. They must ask the right questions. In bankruptcy, you are legally required to disclose all of your assets and where they are and what they are worth. You are required to sign that declaration under oath under penalty of perjury.

The following is a real example from our law practice. On two separate occasions, ladies in their mid-to-late fifties who earned about $40,000 per year had shown up at the office to discuss their financial affairs. Each had accumulated about $250,000 in indebtedness that she could not possibly repay in full. Each sought advice about whether she should file a Chapter 7 bankruptcy. An examination of their affairs reflected that each owned $100,000 to $200,000 in precious jewelry. One lady had inherited the jewelry from her mother and sister, and the other lady had received hers from her late husband many years before.

For those ladies and people in a similar situation, bankruptcy is a very bad option. Their creditors do not know about that valuable jewelry. Under state law, those ladies had no affirmative obligation to tell them about their jewelry. To find out that information, their creditors must first sue them, get judgments, serve them with post-judgment discovery, and ask the right questions. All of that costs money and takes time. As long their creditors don't know about the jewelry, they may decide to cut their losses and leave those ladies alone. The chances are good that the creditors will never find out.

In bankruptcy, these two ladies would be required to disclose their jewelry to the trustee and to their creditors. The penalties for failing to do so are harsh. If either of those ladies failed to disclose the jewelry and someone finds out, she will lose her discharge in bankruptcy and potentially face criminal prosecution for perjury. If those ladies complied with their legal obligations in bankruptcy, they would get a discharge, but they would lose most of the jewelry. The exemption on that jewelry is $7,500 under Texas law or $15,000 if she is married or supporting dependents. In most states, the exemption will be lower. Those ladies are probably better off taking their chances outside of bankruptcy.

Because of the affirmative obligation to disclose what you have, people with valuable non-real estate assets are often poor candidates for bankruptcy.

The decision to file bankruptcy is often a complicated one, with significant advantages and disadvantages, depending upon individual circumstances. Under any circumstances, bankruptcy is a very serious matter. It's like coronary bypass surgery. It can save your life, but you want to avoid it unless the alternatives are clearly worse. Anyone with substantial assets is far better served by having an appropriate asset-protection plan in place, with the ink dry, before the controversy fully arises between that individual and his or her creditors.

⭑ 10 ⭑

How Safe Is Your Safe Haven? Protecting Your Assets in a Foreign Country

No adequate discussion of asset protection could possibly be complete without mention of the science of putting your assets in a very foreign locale where your very angry creditors cannot reach them. A great deal of the material found on the Internet touts the invincibility of a foreign asset-protection trust or, more recently, a foreign limited liability company that could be attacked only through a charging order because the debtor-haven jurisdictions have enacted statutes that so provide. Many faraway places advertise, directly or indirectly, through asset-protection guides and practitioners that assets deposited within those jurisdictions are safe from your creditors, no matter how angry or well-financed they may be.

Spin through related publications, both digital and written solicitations, and you will discover the virtues of accessing those who can help in, for example, Nevis, the

Marshall Islands, Anguilla, the Isle of Man, or the Cook Islands. Just for your information, should you decide to pay a visit, here are the locations of these outposts:

» Nevis is a tiny Caribbean island that is chiefly noted as being the birthplace of Alexander Hamilton.

» The Marshall Islands, of some World War II fame, are north and east of Australia in the Pacific Ocean.

» Anguilla is a speck of an island in the West Indies between the Virgin Islands and the Netherland Antilles.

» The Isle of Man is located between England and Ireland in the Irish Sea. It was once famous for anonymous bank accounts and the saying, "No one will ever know it's your money." For many reasons, the Isle of Man is no longer very helpful—partially because the obliging depository sometimes also forgets that the money belongs to you.

» The Cook Islands are located in the South Pacific between Tahiti and American Samoa.

In all these debtor havens, it is actually very hard for a creditor, no matter how angry, to go—personally or by counsel—and grab assets held far away in a foreign asset-protection trust (FAPT) or a foreign limited liability company that can be subjected only to the charging order procedure adopted in the jurisdiction. It sounds great so far.

But there are very significant limitations that are essentially controlled by the timing of real events. Usually persons who create a FAPT had more than a slight inkling that economic trouble was on the horizon. The debtor knew or strongly suspected something. His business was failing or was about to be made obsolete by technology. He had given an unfortunate guarantee of the financial commitments of the daughter and son-in-law or whatever. He knows or he fears and, for these purposes the two are about the same, that the wolf is coming to the door.

Let's call our financially stressed friend Joe. He quietly asks his lawyer and a few more advisors what he might do with his assets to protect them against loss. He is not encouraged by what he hears. At least for now, what Joe has in mind is not criminal, but it's also not very promising. His first idea was to "give" some assets to a couple of close friends or to change the title to things of value. These are commonplace ideas but not a solution. What's fundamentally wrong is the concept within the American judicial system at all levels of a fraudulent transfer. Joe is, regrettably, informed by his advisors that a transfer of property with intent to defraud creditors is a fraudulent transfer and the recipient can and will be forced to pay Joe's creditors.

The law is unmistakable. When someone owes a lot of money and, after the time when he knows or should have known that he would incur that obligation, if he transfers assets to put them beyond the reach of his creditors, the creditors can get the assets back. There is a presumption of an intention to hinder, delay, and defraud creditors that is almost impossible to refute if, as in Joe's case, the thunder clouds were already in the sky. If bankruptcy is commenced, whether by a voluntary petition by Joe or by an involuntary petition by his creditors, the trustee in bankruptcy can get all the transferred property back. Fraudulent transfer is the cloud over most home-cooked asset-protection schemes.

Joe accepts what he has been told, but he is not yet ready to call his creditors together and hand them his nonexempt assets. He continues to search for a solution and, in these days and times, he turns to that immense source of knowledge and wisdom, the Internet. He seeks an answer to a defined problem: "How may I, without committing a crime, put my assets somewhere my creditors can't get them or at least where he can't get them without a hell of a fight?" As stated, Joe did not institute an asset-protection plan before he knew or had reason to know about the issues that probably would make him seriously indebted to others.

What can he do? Evasion can be useful if guided by very competent counsel. Take every piece of real estate out of Joe's name. Use separate entities, always attaching an LLC after each one. Play for time; don't pray for mercy. Change banks—put the money in the name of your wife or, better yet, your married daughter in Iowa. Make nothing easy—then make a fair offer as an alternative to bankruptcy.

— 11 —

If You Don't Have One, Get One: A Modest Asset Protection Plan

If you have had the opportunity to purchase or otherwise become acquainted with a fully documented asset-protection plan, you were likely bewildered by the number and length of the documents. This chapter identifies the principal elements of the usual, fully documented plan and defines the constituent elements. With these elements clarified, the choice will be made much simpler for you.

The first step is to identify the aggressor. Suppose through a gross miscarriage of justice someone has obtained a final judgment against a guy named Sam for $1 million. A final judgment means just that. All of Sam's rights of appeal or further appeal have expired. He owes a very unfriendly creditor $1 million. We know what the creditor can do to Sam. The sheriff arrives to catalogue nonexempt property. A garnishment is presented at Sam's bank that is intended to capture all the money in his accounts. Post-judgment discovery arrives demanding "tell us what you own and what you owned on the date our lawsuit against you was filed."

Is bankruptcy the only alternative? It might have been but for a suggestion made to Sam by his brother, Jim. Three years before the events that resulted in the judgment, Jim said, "There's this thing called a limited liability company; it's not expensive, and you should get one or two and put your assets in them. It's just better that way—I don't really know why."

At a total cost of $3,600, including filing fees, Joe's tennis partner George, a competent lawyer, formed Sam's Watches and Guns, LLC and Sam's Enterprises, LLC. Sam collected, bought, and traded fine watches. He liked it and was good at it. He also financed car dealers by floor planning expensive cars, and he was pretty good at that. The documentation for each LLC was simple. Here is a summary of what was done:

» Sam's Watches and Guns is organized under the Texas Limited Liability Company Act.

» Sam and his wife are the only owners.

» Ownership shall be measured in "membership interests."

» The original member(s) may admit new members.

» No membership interest may be transferred without the consent of all members.

» A member cannot withdraw from the company.

» There will be an annual meeting.

» No membership may be transferred without the consent of all members.

» The key provisions must not be overlooked.

» If you die, your interest can pass by your will, but the company can buy it back.

» Those who have promised to contribute capital or capital assets, such as expensive watches, must do so.

» There are many tax provisions, most of which are relatively common and in accord with accepted tax law.

» The managers have the power to manage the LLC.

» If a member becomes bankrupt, the company can buy back his interest at fair market value determined by agreement among the insiders of the LLC.

You do not need a law degree to understand that such an agreement makes it very hard for a creditor to reach Sam's assets whether they are watches and guns or cars or loans against cars. That's the purpose of the agreement.

A decent draftsman will capture the essence of this in fifteen pages entitled, "Regulations of Sam's Watches and Guns, LLC." If your plan is drafted by a certain noted attorney, it might run forty to fifty pages. Excessive length is really no crime, but excessive legal charges for long, long documents are a fair criticism of some lawyers.

All of this is to express the remarkable protective characteristics of the Texas Limited Liability Company. Formed in advance of trouble, the LLC protects assets. Creditors cannot reach those assets directly. A limited liability company can own real estate or patents or anything else.

There is an old advertising slogan that says, "If you don't have one, get one." I would add to this slogan as it applies to limited liability companies: "Maybe get two, maybe more, sometimes combined with or used in parallel with a family limited partnership."

A family limited partnership (FLP) is a time-honored method for protecting assets from seizure under writs of execution or attachments. If the assets were placed in the limited partnership before the liability arose to the creditor, the assets are mostly safe. They belong to the FLP that is frequently established for a specific term of years—say ninety years, which is not uncommon. The creditor does not become a creditor of the limited partner in the stead of his debtor because the articles of limited partnership prohibit it. There can be no new limited partners without the consent of all partners.

A family limited partnership standing alone does have vulnerabilities, however. Creditors may attack the general partner who is indebted to them and try to seize his interest. That is pretty tough because most family limited partnership documents prohibit it, but seizure is not totally impossible. There's an answer. Make a limited-liability company the general partner, and make its manager a totally inert—which means not engaged in any business—corporation or other limited liability company.

This chapter highlights the choices of entities that you should utilize as the titleholder for your things of value. When you sell a venture, the proceeds, net of tax, should be retained in your limited partnership and managed at all times by your limited liability company. Suppose, however, you have decided to go into a new venture. You have spotted a great new trend—permanently imprinting on all one's personal clothing an indelible personal identification so laundries and dry cleaners do not have to provide you with personal service across the counter to accept your clothes for care. You just throw them in a bin, they are read electronically, and you pick them up two days later. The recognition equipment is inexpensive, the cleaner's job is much easier, and all are in order for a big payday. But you need $500,000 in outside funds to tie up the prototype and open three locations. You just form a limited partnership and sell limited-partner interests to investors.

Can you use a limited partnership in a protection against any and all future claims? Unfortunately you cannot. If you raise money from investors, the limited partnership will not protect you against their claims for refund of their money when it turns out after the investor funds are spent that your enterprise violated three international patents. As Texas's almost forever governor, Rick Perry, once famously said, "Oops!" And, unfortunately again, selling someone an interest in a limited partnership constitutes the sale of a security under both the Securities Act of the United States and the Texas Securities Act. Your erstwhile partners need show only that the investment as represented to them contained false or misleading information. Failing to tell them that the enterprise would be legally enjoined or prohibited is a material omission by almost anyone's standards, even if, as was true, you didn't know it. Ultimately you will owe them their money.

Waltzing Across the Legal Landscape: Legalese for Asset Protection

One of the failings of my profession, though not the only one, is the perception that everyone you talk to, including clients who are paying for your advice, fully understands the terms you use. Because that is seldom true, this chapter defines some of the more common ones. If you hold a law degree, you can probably skip this section.

Imagine that you, the "judgment debtor" (JD), are currently bothered by a "judgment creditor" (JC) who has come into being after you have adopted the measures recommended here, including both measures tailored to the exemption laws of your particular state. The concentration is on Texas because it is where I live, and because Texas is the poster child for providing personal exemptions to its residents to make life difficult for their judgment creditors. Some, but not all, of the tactics and techniques that are discussed are effective against a JC who pre-exists the date of your adoption of those protections, but it is the cardinal rule of asset protection that doing it ahead of the time that a JC sues you is far preferable to having to construct your plan after the lawsuit has been filed.

Here are a few useful definitions:

Asset Protection—This term means the deliberate, written, legally effective ordering of one's financial affairs so as to provide maximum protection against the collection efforts of a future holder of a judgment against you. In practice, your asset protection plan will include at least one family limited partnership and several limited liability companies, all together sometimes termed the artificial entities. The purpose of asset protection is to make it as difficult, as expensive, and as time consuming as possible within the law for a judgment creditor to obtain value from your assets.

Charging Order—There are several variations of a charging order in practice, but it refers to the legal right to obtain from an artificial entity, such as a limited partnership or a limited liability company, those distributions that are made to you, the JD, which come as a result of your ownership interests but not as a result of the services that you may render to the entity and for which you are compensated with a salary. What is significant about a charging order is that it is the exclusive right to obtain recourse against a JD stemming from that JD's ownership in an artificial entity such as a limited partnership or a limited liability company. A legal conflict is frequently waged between the charging order addressed to the debtor's interest that would properly capture the debtor's right to a distribution of cash proceeds attributable to ownership of that artificial entity but not compensation for services. Major conflicts can arise here because a lot of money is crossing the table. If the debtor actually runs the limited liability partnership or limited liability company, payment for services is reasonable to a point, but when is that point? If the LLC just sold a vacant piece of land and distributed the net proceeds, it's a harder argument that payment was for services, but the necessity to utilize a charging order rather than a direct claim to the assets of a family limited partnership or a limited liability company is the bedrock of asset protection in Texas and all other states with similar jurisprudence. The charging order is discussed further in Chapter 13.

Depositions and Interrogatories—A creditor, after a judgment is obtained, may require his debtor to answer questions under oath about his financial affairs. It's usually a game of cat and mouse, the creditors trying to ask the right questions and the debtor trying to avoid answering without actually lying under oath. Some debtors are naturally gifted to play this game.

Execution—An execution occurs when a judgment creditor uses a sheriff, constable, or US Marshall to go out and seize your nonexempt personal property for the purpose of selling it in full or partial reduction of the indebtedness owed to the JC. Despite the onerous sound of the term, you do not lose your life, only your assets.

Statutory Exemption—This exemption is a declaration by state law that some asset that you have or may acquire will be safe from the reach of a future judgment creditor. Texas's list of exemptions is very important to Texas residents. Every other state provides a certain degree of exemptions, but the Texas list is the longest and the most effective.

Fraudulent Transfer—A fraudulent transfer is a determination by a judgment that a debtor intentionally placed assets beyond the immediate reach of a creditor. If after a drunk-driving episode, the driver transfers all his assets out of this country, under whatever legal guise; that is highly likely to be determined later to have been a fraudulent transfer. Fraudulent transfers may be avoided, which means forced to be repaid to creditors under both state law and the federal laws pertaining to bankruptcy.

Garnishment—A garnishment means a judgment a creditor may get a legal writ that authorizes garnishing or seizing any bank account that you may have or order any party that may owe you money to turn it over to the JC to satisfy the debt. For example, a JC may garnish your monthly royalty check from Barnett Shale production or your right to receive money on a regular basis from any other source that is obligated to make such payments. In Texas, however, your salary derived from work which you do and certain other receipts may not be garnished; that is an important right under the category known as exemptions.

Inception—Inception is a legal term, sometimes hard to understand when considered in the debtor and creditor context. It is often misunderstood. The inception of a financial event is that time when it became more likely than less likely that the adverse financial event would occur. You need to choose and complete your asset protection plan before the inception of a highly adverse financial setback. For example, if you, after a few too many drinks, are involved in an automobile accident causing serious injury to someone, the accident is the inception of the event that may later lead to a huge judgment against you even though the actual lawsuit may be filed fourteen months later. The reason inception is so important is that it bears on fraudulent transfer. Transfers of assets after the inception of what proves to be a large financial setback brings the doctrine of fraudulent transfer into play. The later the transfer occurs, the worse for you.

Judgment—A judgment is an order of a court of competent jurisdiction, which means that a proper court had the right to issue a judgment against you, declaring that a party is entitled to recover from you a specific sum of money, plus continuing interest. The party holding such a judgment is known as a JC. A final judgment means a judgment that cannot be further appealed. Most judgments employed in a collection process are final judgments. There are risks to a creditor who acts on a judgment subject to appeal. Unless you post a bond, however, a creditor can seek to collect from you while the judgment is on appeal. A JC has the benefit of a certain number of rights and practices to enable him to collect his judgment against you.

So that's the tension. Imagine someone holds a final judgment against you, a citizen of Texas, and is trying to collect $100,000. Before the inception of the events giving rise to that judgment, you reasonably employed adequate counsel, utilized your Texas exemptions, formed a series of connected artificial entities that provide protection against a potential JC, and have so conducted your affairs as to keep those entities alive and vital for the purpose of providing you a defense against a JC. The claim against you will be settled. You may pay more than you believe you deserved to pay, but you will make that deal and move on.

In an alternate circumstance, suppose that you failed to establish an asset protection plan, despite the fact that

I went to this length to persuade you to do so. The good news is that you are a resident of the Lone Star State. The bad news is that you guaranteed certain bank obligations, a lot of them, present and future, of an equity fund managed by your old college roommate and continuing best friend who raised a $50-million investment fund, based on his amazing record of stock market success in trading in international prescription drug companies. Successful he was. Honest, sadly, he was not. His successes were based on insider information regarding drug successes and failures, as well as advance knowledge of the imminent announcements of new drugs that were better and cheaper than some old favorites. The tipsters folded under federal prosecution and told all. It was not a pretty story. At the end of the day, the bank seems to have lost $10 million and is looking in your direction. They haven't acted yet, but they are sure to do so. You seek your counsel's advice.

At length, decisions are made. You are clearly not implicated in any criminal activity. That's good. You also did not receive any distributions from the fund. That's good, but even $2 million will absolutely wipe you out. Your astute counsel learns something else of interest. The bank has some captured assets; it will make some recovery, but more importantly, you are likely to get a short breathing spell before being sued.

What should you do? You and your lawyer turn to that old standby—the unlimited Texas homestead exemption. You find a house that is well located in a great place to live. You buy it, converting many, if not all, of your nonexempt assets, including cash, your present house, some small royalties, and three investment properties into a huge down payment on your new homestead. At closing, you pay $2,250,000, which results in a small mortgage. You also align your automobile ownership and other assets to conform to the Texas exemptions, and then you wait.

The bank sends a demand letter. You respond by stating that you have no assets subject to execution, that you believe the fools at the bank were negligent and damaged you, but that you will borrow $25,000 from your brother and offer it as full settlement. The game is on. The bank investigates. They say you liquidated nonexempt assets to buy an expensive house.

You say, "So what?"

They say, "Our general counsel in Atlanta says that is a fraudulent transfer."

Your lawyer says "Not in Texas. One may acquire an exempt homestead at any time. And one may use otherwise nonexempt assets to do it."

Is he right? Most of us think he is.

Now, it's clear that if the bank forces you into bankruptcy, your Texas homestead exemption will fail to the extent that you used nonexempt assets to buy it. But banks do not like to enter bankruptcy court. If you are current on all other obligations, the bank will be very reluctant to file an involuntary petition against you. The penalties for doing so wrongfully are severe. And there may be rumors that the bank got treated better than the investors. Bankruptcy is a risky option for the bank.

What will happen next? After spitting at each other for a while, the parties will settle. This is not, by far, as advantageous as if you had completed a competent asset protection plan before anyone, including you, knew your old roommate was a crook, but it is a settlement nonetheless. Remember that the settlement is made a little sweeter by the fact that your new home has appreciated substantially during the time involved in the disputes.

None of this was fun. None of it compares to having a proper asset protection plan in place before adversity strikes. Mostly that's the reason creditors confronted by a proper APP are limited in the remedies. They must deal with the charging order.

Making Davy Crockett Proud: Defining the Scope of the Charging Order

The moment has come to discuss the charging order—what it is and what it is not. As a potential debtor, someone who owes or may come to owe money to someone else, wave your Lone Star flag. The Texas statute governing Texas law of limited liability companies could hardly be improved. Beware, however, that if you do business in another state and become indebted under the laws of that state, particularly to a resident of that state, your protections under the Texas statute may be limited or erased. Make it a point to confine your activities to Texas and your obligation to personal and corporate residents of Texas. Even if you don't, the charging order is very useful.

A charging order started with the British Partnership Act as a mechanism to prevent the judgment creditor of a partner from invading the partnership and grabbing its assets as satisfaction for one partner's debt. In the nineteenth century, the English venerated the partner-ship. Most financial institutions, even the famous family groups, such as the Rothchilds, were organized as partnerships. They needed protection, and parliament awarded it. Over time, this happy concept was carried forward into American law in the form of the Uniform Partnership Act. You might enjoy a well-written article, "Recent Developments in Charging Orders" from the February 2013 publication *Business Law Today*.

In the 1990s, state legislatures authorized the creation of limited liability companies, which operate like partnerships but provide the protection of limited liability for the owners without some of the drawbacks of traditional partnerships.

The Texas Statute appears at § 101.112 of the Texas Business Organization Code. That section is entitled "Member's Membership Interest Subject to Charging Order." I hate technical discussion of statutes and learned treatises, but unfortunately to understand asset protection, you have to understand not only what charging orders do but, more importantly, what they stop others from doing. Here are the highlights under Texas law:

A charging order is the exclusive remedy in Texas for seeking payment of a judgment against a member of a LLC. It does not affect a judgment against the LLC itself.

If a creditor gets a charging order, which is granted by a district judge, he is only entitled to intercept and receive distributions to an individual member, when and if made. Stop there. An individual member may be an employee and may be the sole employee of the LLC. If so, he may be paid a reasonable salary, including a bonus, for services and stellar performance in the opinion of the manager of the LLC, who might also be the judgment debtor. Compensation for services rendered is salary in Texas and is exempt from execution at the moment of payment.

Your LLC may need more than one member. Some state courts, such as Florida, have denied the protections of an LLC to a single-member LLC, reasoning that protection of a partnership is not appropriate when there is only one member. As a matter of logic, a partnership requires at least two partners. It's an interesting philosophical question; don't pay fancy lawyers to have it decided in your case. Just have two or more members.

Some states allow a judgment creditor to obtain a lien on and ultimately foreclose on a membership interest. Texas, emphatically, does not. The charging lien is all the creditor gets.

To add insult to injury, a judgment creditor cannot demand an audit or even see the books and records of the LLC. He is not a member, historically, a position akin to partner, and outsiders do not get access to partnership records. Note that the judgment creditor can get a judgment lien on a member's interest, but he can't do anything with it unless the member tries to sell it, and this is not likely.

The statute says it again—the charging order, as described, is the sole remedy under Texas law that can affect an interest owned by a member in a Texas Limited Liability Company. To grasp further the significance of the benefits of a Texas Limited Partnership or Limited Liability Company, it is important to understand that neither the general partner of a family limited partnership nor the manager of a limited liability company is required to make any distributions to an owner in respect of his percentage of ownership. It is equally important to understand that when you do business as a partial owner of a limited liability company, you are not legally responsible for making additional contributions to the LLC (as such entities are termed) unless the formation documents of the LLC so state, and you assume that obligation. I advise you not to do that. The corollary to "don't do that" is do not create asset protection entities by following the legal forms available in do-it-yourself books or on the Internet.

The following is a summary of limited liability companies for use in APPs.

Use limited liability companies and use them and use them. Use a different one for every discrete investment. Assume you have sponsored two horses—one that can't run and one that is a Derby winner. That's the nature of speculative investment. Don't let the lame horse drag down the winner. You probably didn't think it was speculative investment, but most great ideas are. Having said this, abide a few cautions.

Always have two or more participants in the LLC, never just one.

» Keep good records.

» Have at least two face-to-face meetings a year with your lawyer or anyone else who is capable of hearing what the enterprise did in the recent past. Then put together competent minutes of the meeting with attached exhibits. Faded ink is better than a good memory.

» Put all the activity history in writing. One page is likely sufficient, plus exhibits. This document will tell the story of a legitimate venture, not a scheme to beat your creditors. Keep the records.

» Get the annual tax forms properly prepared and distributed, particularly if you are drawing money, including a right to a fantastic bonus that I am sure you will earn.

Do it all right and, at least in Texas and most other states, your member's interest in your limited liability companies will be protected from a judgment creditor.

And most importantly to Texans—Davy Crockett will be very proud of you.

— 14 —

Best Little Asset Advice in Texas: Choosing the Right Asset Protection Plan

From now on as you read, assume and act on the proposition that you are interested in at least learning the components of a personalized asset protection plan and how such a plan might benefit you. Consider three questions:

1. What should the plan really do for you?
2. Where should one go for the necessary legal advice?
3. What does the plan cost, now and in the future?

If there is any ultimate truth in this area of endeavor, it is that one size does not fit all. Under that wisdom, there are other guiding principles. These are the basics:

» Start early.
» Design the APP from the bottom up.
» Never place ownership of nonexempt assets in an individual.

To learn now what to do and what not to do, it is necessary to recognize the types of entities that from time to time are promoted as the building blocks of an asset protection plan. Consider the family trust, sometimes termed a living trust. By this instrument, the head of the family or co-heads, if a married couple is participating, declare that certain assets that they previously owned individually shall hereafter be owned by the family trust.

Typically these assets include the house, which is now to be occupied by certain family members while it is owned by the trust. Placing the title of the house in the name of the trust eliminates the likelihood that an occupant with the title in his or her name, as would be the result of an outright gift, will find a way to lose ownership of the house. Such trusts may also dispose of cash or other valuables. The trust also protects the financial misadventures of those benefitted, but the trust does not provide asset protection. If the entrustors or grantors were insolvent before the transfers, they can be avoided, which means set aside by creditors whose claims predate the trust. And so long as individuals are the trustees, they can be reached with legal process. These trusts can, and often do, contain provisions to lessen estate taxes, as well as income taxes by means of a marital trust, sometimes identified as a QTIP trust, with provisions that allow certain limited tax exclusions, such as maximum generation-skipping transfer tax exclusion, but all of that is beyond our review.

As described, the family living trust is a bad choice, and even a family limited partnership, standing alone, provides limited asset protection. It violates the rule that the active decision maker should not be an individual. There is a role, however, for a limited partnership in a better-balanced plan.

In an earlier chapter, you met a man called BT, an American athletic hero, looking for economic action. His smart sister, Lydia, explained to him in some detail and with persuasive skill that he needed a competent asset protection plan now before he got involved in any risky financial ventures, particularly with his new running mates, who she described as a bunch of "flakes." She felt she was being charitable. Follow along these two differing scripts portraying BT's adventures as a first-time-venture capitalist. In the first example, BT, who loves his sister very much, hugged her, thanked her, and forgot about everything she said. In the second script, he carefully followed her advice before making the investments. In both instances, the investments and his partners are identical.

After reviewing about ten proposals advanced to him by his three buddies, BT selected three separate deals. He agreed to back a sports-oriented barbershop in the Houston area. He approved the plans for two locations. He guaranteed an unlimited line of credit with Fourth

National Bank. He believed the cost of the leasehold improvements would not exceed $500,000 per location. He was wrong.

BT forgot about the advance draws that his partners paid themselves. He did not anticipate that the primary colors for the shops would be changed three times or that both the general contractor and the interior designer were closely related to one of the other partners. Actually the idea was not bad, just terribly executed at hugely unreasonable expense. At the end of the day, the shops were sold—the calculated loss, as reflected by the unpaid note at the bank—$1,450,000. He thought he would have to pay one-fourth. He paid almost all of it. Each of his partners made a token contribution to him of $50,000.

He bought 25 percent of a foreign car dealership. He figured it couldn't miss, and besides, he would get great cars cheap. At some point, he learned about something called a floor plan. When the bank called the roll of its collateral, some of the mortgaged cars did not answer. They did not answer for the very good reason that they never existed. Some cars had existed and seemed lost. "Sorry about that," said two of his partners. BT was stuck owing the bank $1.2 million. The other partners paid nothing.

He and the boys backed a fitness center in Houston. Strangely the young couple who ran it were attractive and talented. They worked hard. The center drew members. The presence of former great athletes helped, but BT's partners needed money, really needed money. The other three partners begged BT to sell and get a payday. He went along, and they sold their interest, all of them including BT, for $400,000 and a release from all obligations. BT got a check for $100,000.

BT lost $2.4 million, a substantial amount but happily not a total erasure of BT's net worth. The names have been changed, but I have seen this type of experience more than once. If inexperienced in documenting business transactions and under pressure from a bank collecting in its personal guarantees, the one rich guy will pay 100 percent of the losses when the deals collapse and get 25 percent of the occasional success, assuming four participants, as described. BT should have listened to his sister.

Imagine instead that BT did the smart thing and listened to Lydia, who accompanied him on three visits to a good lawyer. The net result of those three visits was a fully documented and fully complete asset protection plan. He and his wife initiated a family limited partnership managed by a limited liability company. All of their possessions, all cash, everything, except those assets exempt from creditors under Texas statutes, were assigned and transferred by final complete documentation into the family limited partnership. They then formed three LLCs, one for each investment. BT never invested in any deal individually, only through the LLCs chosen for that purpose. Each LLC made a cash contribution to its single venture, exactly as the venture documents provided. The venture documents were reviewed for competency. Each was a corporation owned by BT's limited liability company and his three coventurers. Each corporation, under the strict supervision of his sister, conducted all necessary legal formalities; its valid existence could not be challenged.

What about those guarantees? When the businesses failed, each bank, through eminent counsel, knocked on BT's door. The first knock was polite, but the next was not so polite. They asked and then demanded that he pay all of the calculated debt. He said no and explained why. He raised this one issue—both banks had prior, somewhat unsatisfactory lending experience with each of the other participants. They had been paid back, but the processes were acrimonious. BT remembered that each senior banker had welcomed the four investors and said wonderful things about BT's newfound friends. Is that a legal defense? Probably not, but it's better than nothing.

What was far better than nothing was that BT had no significant assets subject to legal exposure. Everything was exempt or in a protected entity. The banks could get a charging order against the Family Limited Partnership or each separate LLC. Good luck with that! But BT's sister and her lawyer friend were not silent participants. Essentially they said to the banks that while they had good legal defenses, and that they believed the approving banker had taken bribes in the nature of continued golf course winnings from BT's partners, nonetheless BT would match what they collected from all three other guarantors.

The banks said, "Hell, no!"

Lydia suggested BT's answer to that. He said, "Adios."

The banks looked at their hole cards, and then they jumped all over the other three guarantors—false and fraudulent financial statements—the whole nine yards. At the end of the day, the three *amigos* very reluctantly paid a total of $400,000. To resolve the situation, BT exceeded his final offer and paid $750,000, and the matter was closed as to all parties. Paying $750,000 at eighteen months is a lot better than $2.4 million right now. That's what a solid, timely asset protection plan can do. It's not a get-out-of-jail-free card. The debtor doesn't thumb his nose and walk away. To the largest extent possible, he participates in a solution somewhat fair to all.

How did BT, with a little help from his knowledge-able attorney, actually structure his affairs, in advance of making these speculative investments? You will see his asset protection plan (APP) in the exhibit on page 116. Note the distinctive features of the organizational plan:

1. All major family assets are owned by the Family Limited Partnership.

2. No significant assets are owned by BT or his wife, individually.

3. Each investment is made by a separate Limited Liability Company.

4. All entity managers are separate Limited Liability Companies.

The key is to organize one's affairs before any major financial calamity.

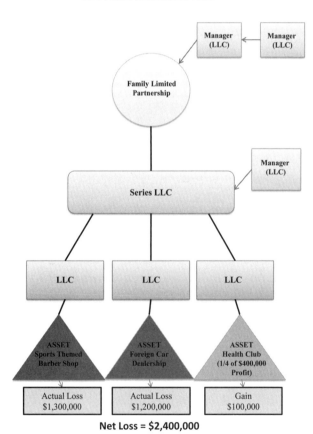

BT's Asset Protection Plan

In another situation, BT, his brilliant sister Lydia, and his sagacious Aunt Matilda, a long-time, much-honored schoolteacher, decided to invest in a project together. Lydia and Matilda noticed that almost all of Matilda's students were totally connected electronically and used computers effortlessly to handle most of life's everyday communication problems. Persons over the age of forty were not and did not. They decided to make everyday living easier for the noncomputer literate. What is important for our purposes is that BT was not burned out on investing. He had lost some money, but he had plenty left, and he had learned.

First and foremost, even at the advent of what appears to be a small risk, he realized he should limit economic exposure. He had created and now would utilize a competent APP. BT had total confidence in Lydia, and he certainly should have. This time, BT requested a budget and asked questions. How long does it take to produce a working model? How shall we try to sell it or license it? Who is our first prospect? When those questions were answered to his satisfaction, he caused a limited liability company to be created, obtained a trademark of the name Easy Chair, and put $50,000 in a bank account. The manager of the new LLC was another limited liability company.

The Easy Chair concept was easy to explain. It involved a walk-in computer service, complete with a competent technician in a very convenient location.

The serviceperson would assist the customer in paying bills, registering cars, paying taxes, researching competitive providers of energy, home improvements, plumbers, health care, and the rest of life's everyday needs that necessarily involve other persons and can be accessed and investigated with electronic capabilities. They presented their idea to a friend, the manager of a local Radio Shack store in Houston.

Radio Shack's retail network includes more than 4,000 stores in the United States. About two-thirds of America's population lives conveniently near a Radio Shack store. And Radio Shack needed new ideas. It really did. Its first and second quarters, as reported to investors, were deplorable financial results. Gross profit declined; it showed an operating loss and large net losses. The new chief executive, the latest of many, said things would get better. No one believed him.

Yet fate played a role. The Houston store manager who was first contacted by Lydia and Matilda was well-connected. He understood electronic communications and was highly regarded in the company. He liked the idea of having Easy Chairs in Radio Shack stores, and he knew where to take it. It is said that "nothing succeeds like success." It is equally true that failure creates a need to act, to do something different. Amazingly, within a very bureaucratic company, he got permission to put in his store a four-desk complex of Easy Chairs.

Current Radio Shack employees were fully capable of manning the posts—it wasn't as impressive as an Apple store, but for Radio Shack it was new, different, and exciting. The service employees loved it. It was far better than standing around waiting on sales magically to pick up. They originally charged twenty-five dollars per hour and then raised the charge to fifty dollars per hour with a twenty-five dollar minimum.

Traffic increased and increased. They went to an appointment system and then added two more desks, which then covered all the room they had. The concept spread, Radio Shack acquired all of the intellectual property and set up a royalty system payable to BT's family. The rest is history. BT made $1.5 million buying calls or options on Radio Shack stock. Radio Shack is real. The balance of this tale is illustrative but imaginary.

The moral of this tale is that good ideas still mean something. If you are determined to invest, plan your investments properly. Determine what sum you are willing to risk. If you must, because you still like the deal, invest more cash; do so, but never, ever become personally responsible for the activities of the enterprise. The stand-alone LLC is your investment vehicle of choice.

A final but necessary word: Choose your partners with as much care as you chose your spouse. Another honored adage: "There are no good deals with bad partners." This adage is sad but true, particularly if you are the only partner with real money. What happens all too often is that the enterprise has not found success, but you have invested all you are willing to put into it. No one else steps up. Then you learn that your partners have assured certain creditors that they need not worry about their invoices because you, their rich partner, will take care of it. Naturally they forgot to tell you about this reassuring conversation. When failure arrives, the doors are shut, and a lot of people are very mad at you. The only way to avoid all this aggravation, as well as partners who dip into the till, is to choose them with great care and carefully document your financial commitment. If you think you need to watch your partners to be sure they don't steal, don't do the deal with those partners.

One of the problems connected with advising clients regarding asset protection is that they sometimes ask, not surprisingly, "Do you think I should make this investment?" My answer that I haven't the slightest idea has not been well received. Long ago, I developed a sort of qualified response. If I don't know anything about the intended investment, I don't just guess. That would be a disservice to put it mildly, and it might be something I would later deeply regret.

The response I give to the question of whether or not to make an investment is not so much an answer as it is a cautionary tale. I simply relate the tale of my own small business investment experience. I have invested in local real estate under the guidance of my wife, a talented real estate broker and investment advisor. We have generally been successful in these deals, which is not terribly surprising because the Dallas–Fort Worth area has been and continues to be one of America's fastest-growing regions.

On the other hand, as all economists learn to say, my more individualistic investments have not been glorious. My doctor, a very close friend, and I invested in developing "Fun Palaces," which were pinball and foosball parlors located near area high schools. Unfortunately the unexpected, rampant, and growing drug culture wiped us out. We didn't think of that.

And I, always fascinated by the carnival business, invested with friends in the invention and development of two amusement rides to be sold to touring carnivals. The nicest way to sum up our experience is to say we manufactured two types of rides: one cost more than we could sell it for, and the other never worked properly.

From the telling of my investment history, I extrapolate to my clients. First, I tell them to make sure they understand the industry they are targeting. Is it changing? Why aren't people already doing what you want to invest in doing? To what extent is the deal dependent on any mechanism not yet perfected? I have found this caution to be helpful to some ready-to-go investors. Stopping and thinking is a useful exercise. For my part, I did not recommend or disparage anything.

If you have decided to make a speculative investment, follow all the rules:

» Invest what you can afford to lose.

» Understand the consequences of inducing others to invest with you, including mutual investments in a limited partnership.

» Make no personal guarantees.

» Know your partner(s).

» Utilize nothing but limited liability companies as investment vehicles.

» Engage a competent lawyer early even if, or maybe because, he lacks an entrepreneurial spirit.

» Be lucky or very well prepared.

~ 15 ~

Do-Si-Do with Your Best Partner: How to Choose a Lawyer and Estimate Legal Costs

Most all of the lawyers I know who practice in this space—pure asset protection, estate planning and asset protection, and bankruptcy—are honest, ethical, and smart. That doesn't mean any particular lawyer is right for you. So who is best for you? Proper selection is better understood by identifying possible disqualifying factors rather than by trying to identify the single, very best one.

There are many factors to keep in mind when looking for a lawyer to help you prepare an asset protection plan. One suggestion is to avoid using family members or someone closely related to a family member. Yes, they may be cheaper and just as smart, but you may not be as comfortable opening your financial kimono to someone considered in the family.

Be mindful that tax planning, which is the essence of most intricate estate planning, is not asset protection by a different name. Prominent estate planners tend to be very expensive and to provide a work product that far, far exceeds your actual desire or need for a workable flexible asset protection plan. Treat potential tax issues as a different subject.

Choosing a lawyer based on age or sex is not recommended either. Gray hair or no hair, attractive or not, is no assurance of competence and diligence and, most importantly, the ability to communicate with you. Good lawyers are good lawyers. Ask around. The same five or so names will likely surface unless you live in Dallas or Houston where the talent pool is deeper.

Make your first visit an interview. You are the one who will choose. Be open about what assets you have and what you want to achieve. Your conversation with the lawyer is confidential—it really is—don't worry about what you confide unless it relates to criminal behavior, and you don't do that.

Finally be entirely prepared to walk out or just not return. If the connection doesn't feel right, he or she, no matter how talented, may not be the lawyer for you. But play it straight. Tell the lawyer you are not ready at this time to commit your business to him or her, but please, please offer to pay for the lawyer's time. He or she may not accept your offer, but do what is right and make the offer. And as often occurs, after visiting with more lawyers, if you like the first lawyer best, be sure the door is fully open for you to return and make that selection. Once you have found a lawyer, what should you expect?

The most efficient summary of written asset protec tion instruments includes a family limited partnership, managed by a limited liability company and separate limited liability companies for each enterprise or undertaking that may give rise to financial risk. As an added layer of protection, I believe that each LLC that you utilize to conduct an active enterprise should itself be managed by a separate LLC. No individual human hands on any wheel.

Historically it was expensive to form a Texas LLC, but an amendment to the Texas Statute allows the for-mation of a series LLC that greatly reduces the initial cost of forming these different legal enterprises. There are other states offering this option now too. One series might include only the active fronting LLCs. The one other series might include managers for all the active LLCs. This sounds more complicated than it is, and it really is the best way to limit risk. Your lawyer will walk you through it in the time span of one meeting.

An example of a series LLC is the business plan of Robert Smith and wife Sandy who own and operate seven tanning salons. Tanning is a controversial process. In most cases, tanning salons are legal, but there seem to be dangers. The Smiths, however, have done well in the tanning business. They have cash reserves, invest-ments in stocks and bonds, a vacation home in Hawaii, and local investments in real estate. All of that, together with all jewelry and other collectibles of value, such as paintings and antiques, should be owned by their family limited partnership. And a family-owned limited liability company must be the general partner.

How about the tanning shops? Ideally each one should be a separate LLC. Because of the series LLC laws, it's not much more expensive than just one operating LLC, and it gives much more protection. If someone claims to have lost hair or sexual prowess in the tanning process, the claim is limited to one LLC. The owners may decide to shut that store down, even if insured, rather than spend years fighting the claim. The evils of tanning are a known risk; there is no legal reason why the owners can't wall off the separate locations. And they should.

This practice is instructional. Every separate economic activity that has historical risk should be in a separate limited liability company. This includes your incredible art collection, if you buy and sell art, even infrequently; your investment in a children's baseball learning facility with batting cages; and your wife's investment in a franchised distribution of cosmetics or general nutrition products. The list is long; ours is a litigious society.

With that as background, now study the provisions of the two basic agreements, the family limited partnership and the limited liability company. In the appendix, you will find such documents—names changed and all identifying special provisions deleted—of two agreements in use by clients of this office. The family names of husband and wife have been deleted and replaced by two wonderful persons in Texas history: James "Pa" Ferguson and his more celebrated wife, Miriam "Ma" Ferguson. Each person served as governor of Texas: Pa served once, and Ma served twice. Theirs is a great story; however, they did not form a Texas Limited Partnership, and unfortunately, I did not have the opportunity to represent them in any legal matter. I just used their names for fun. People like Ma and Pa Ferguson and their daughters need to be remembered.

The process around the creation of an asset protection plan is a lot to learn in a hurry. Please review the key provisions below before jumping into these legal documents. However, the following description should be enough to give you the general concept. The road map will help. And I very much hope you do not decide to prepare your own documents. Remember: "A lawyer who represents himself has a fool for counsel." Have these documents prepared and routinely administered by lawyers who know how to handle such business.

The Texas Limited Partnership
Key provisions:
» Names of the general partner and all limited partners

- Adoption of the Texas statutes re limited partnerships
- A boring list of definitions
- Location of business, name of registered agent
- Purposes, generally everything lawful under the sun
- Capital contribution
- Ownership of assets in name of partnership
- Authority of general partner—limitations on such authority
- Nomination of tax partner
- Limitation on powers of limited partners
- Who owns what
- Transfers of interest—note heavy restriction
- Pricing interests
- How interests may be sold
- Admission of new partners (very restricted)
- Accounting matters
- Everyone's affirmations that they understand that this is a limited partnership

The Texas Limited Liability Company

- Names of parties involved
- Formation under Texas Limited Liability Statute
- Membership—disposition of interests (very restrictive)
- Rights of assignees (very few)
- Ban on encumbrances (i.e., liens on interests)

» Capital contributions and failure to pay
» Management by managers
» Limitations on liability of the managers
» Tax policies
» Winding up

The Texas Liability Company law prohibits anyone from directly acquiring a member's interest by legal process. All a creditor can get is a charging order, which you now understand is a long way from a powerful weapon. And that's the reason folks form Texas Limited Liability Companies.

Visualize yourselves. You and your spouse are sitting in your newly chosen lawyer's office. Assume you presently have no entities of the nature described, but you and your spouse have been successful and own assets of all types worth $4 million in presumed fair market value.

Where do you go from here? You worry the clock is ticking; you know that lawyers' clocks run faster than any others because lawyers bill by the hour. You are already nervous—how much have I spent drinking coffee and talking about the Cowboys who never seem to get any better?

I've estimated the costs below that you can reasonably expect to be charged for the legal process of creating an asset protection plan. You will need two, maybe three, visits to the lawyer's office. In two hours, the attorney will tell you what is needed. You will deliver those documents and records to his paralegal. In the second visit, you will review the documents prepared for your signatures. Some corrections will be required. The third visit will entail reviewing the, hopefully, final documents and signing them with a lot of transfer documents that place the several assets where they should be.

Approximate costs:

First Visit—$1,250.00

First drafts of recommended documents—$2,500.00

Second Visit—Explanations, including what the lawyer(s) got factually wrong—$1,500.00

Third Visit—Full review of what is being done, correction of minor errors in names or descriptions, and signature—$1,500.00

Subtotal—$6,750.00

And also you will pay expenses for recording documents, notifying insurance carriers of name changes, and so on—$1,000 (approximately)

Total: $7,750.00

That's really all it should cost, unless you are Warren T. Buffet or Lindsay Lohan. Special needs require more resources.

⟶ EPILOGUE ⟶

Don't Make This Your Last Rodeo

Asset protection is not predominately a strategy to save taxes, although the conversion from direct ownership of assets to partial ownership of entities is helpful when valuing estates. As we have discussed, you do not need the most celebrated tax lawyer in town. The most celebrated tax lawyer will likely also be the most expensive. A very high legal cost is unnecessary to this purpose. Any good commercial lawyer can draft a fine asset protection plan and see it through successful operation.

Being a smart client really works. If you have read this book or one of many others, you already know generally what you need. Speed up the process and reduce expensive face time with your lawyer and his or her associates. Bring to the first meeting a complete list and description of all the major assets, including legal descriptions, usually in the form of copies of deeds and/or mortgages. Bring copies of certificates of title to all vehicles in excess of your two or more Texas exemptions. Identify who, if not you, should share in management responsibilities. Identify those, if any, who should absolutely not share in management responsibilities. Bring federal income-tax returns for the last two years—things you have forgotten about will be brought back into memory. Do it right, and you may get it all done in two, not three, very constructive visits. Your legal bill will benefit accordingly.

This isn't the end of the process. Actually you never are completely finished with this process, so at this time schedule an annual follow-up visit and review. Laws change and asset composition changes. Children become adults. Some activities have increased in risk; others have been eliminated. Once a year, just like your annual physical, go over all of it with your counsel at a straight hourly rate of say $475.00 per hour, perhaps including at no extra charge his or her paralegal who will take notes on all matters presented, write competent minutes for each important economic activity, and provide you with a to-do list. An obsolete asset protection plan will fail to do its job. The annual review is not an add-on; it's critical to long-term protection.

I am pleased to have spent some time with you. Take care of yourself financially—no one else will.

Appendix A

LIMITED PARTNERSHIP AGREEMENT
OF
FERGUSON FAMILY LIMITED PARTNERSHIP
(A Texas Limited Partnership)

NOTICE: THE INTERESTS EVIDENCED BY THIS AGREEMENT HAVE BEEN ACQUIRED FOR INVESTMENT ONLY AND MAY NOT BE SOLD, TRANSFERRED, OR OFFERED FOR SALE UNTIL SUCH INTERESTS ARE REGISTERED UNDER THE SECURITIES ACT OF 1933 OR OF THE STATE OF TEXAS OR UNLESS EXEMPTIONS FROM THE REGISTRATION REQUIREMENTS OF SUCH ACTS ARE THEN APPLICABLE TO SUCH OFFER OR SALE, AND THE PROVISIONS OF THIS AGREEMENT ARE SATISFIED.

THIS LIMITED PARTNERSHIP AGREEMENT ("Agreement") is made and entered into effective on March 15, 2013, by and between FERGUSON FAMILY GP, L.L.C., a Texas limited liability company, as the "General Partner," and JAMES "PA" FERGUSON and MIRIAM A. "MA" FERGUSON, as the initial "Limited Partners," together with any additional or substituted Partners admitted to the Partnership in accordance with the terms of this Agreement. Unless otherwise specified in this Agreement, "Partner" refers to any individual General Partner or Limited Partner, and "Partners" refers to the General Partner and Limited Partners collectively.

WHEREAS, the Partners desire to form a limited partnership pursuant to the provisions of Chapter 153 of the Texas Business Organizations Code (the "Act") and pursuant to the terms described below; and

WHEREAS, the Partners desire to form a limited partnership for the purposes set forth herein and desire to set forth the terms and conditions with respect to the Partnership operations, the relationships between the Partners and the restrictions regarding the transfer of a Partner's interest in the Partnership.

NOW, THEREFORE, for and in consideration of the formation of the limited partnership, and in further consideration of the mutual covenants and promises herein expressed, the receipt and sufficiency of which are hereby acknowledged, the Partners hereby agree as follows:

Article I
Definitions

1.01 The following terms have the following meanings when used in this Agreement:

"Act" means the Texas Business Organizations Code, Chapter 153, Vernon's Texas Civil Statutes, as enacted and amended from time to time and any successor statutes.

"Affiliate" means any person or entity that controls or is controlled by the General Partner, or is controlled by the same person or entity that controls the General Partner. In this definition, the term "control" includes the ownership of more than fifty percent (50%) of the beneficial interest in the person or entity.

"Agreement" means this Limited Partnership Agreement, including any amendments that may be made from time to time.

"Bankruptcy" means, as to any Partner, the Partner's taking, or acquiescing in the taking, of any action seeking relief under, or advantage of, any applicable debtor relief, liquidation, receivership, conservatorship, bankruptcy, moratorium, rearrangement, insolvency, reorganization or similar law affecting the rights or remedies of creditors generally, as in effect from time to time. For the purpose of this definition, the term "acquiescing" shall include, without limitation, the failure to file, within ten (10) days after its entry, a petition, answer, or motion to vacate or to discharge any order, judgment, or decree providing for any relief under any such law.

"Capital Contribution(s)" means the contribution(s) made to the capital of the Partnership from time to time by a Partner in cash or property.

"Certificate" means the Certificate of Limited Partnership to be filed by the General Partner with the Secretary of State of the State of Texas in accordance with this Agreement.

"Code" means the Internal Revenue Code of 1986, as amended and in effect from time to time (or any corresponding provision or provisions of succeeding law).

"Immediate Family" means any descendant or ancestor of a Partner who is also a lineal descendant. Lineal descendants shall include all adopted and natural children and descendants. Immediate Family shall not include spouses of Partners or spouses of other persons in their Immediate Family.

"Percentage Interest" means the percentage interest of a Partner in the capital and profits and losses of the Partnership. The initial Percentage Interest is set forth in Section 10.02 of this Agreement, subject to subsequent adjustment pursuant to Section 6.07 of this Agreement.

"Person" means an individual, corporation, partnership, trust, unincorporated organization, association, or other entity. "His" or "he" shall also mean and refer, as appropriate, to the feminine and neuter pronouns.

"Required Interest" means one or more of the Limited Partners having among them greater than fifty percent (50%) of the Percentage Interest of all Limited Partners in their capacity as such.

"Transfer" means the mortgage, pledge, hypothecation, transfer, sale, assignment, or other disposition of any part or all of an interest in the Partnership by any Partner, whether voluntarily, by operation of law or otherwise.

The term "Proportionate Share" as applied herein to the portion of the Percentage Interest which a Limited Partner (the "Purchasing Limited Partner") shall have a right or an obligation to purchase hereunder, if at all, means that portion of Percentage Interest then subject to purchase which the Percentage Interest owned by the Purchasing Limited Partner bears to the Percentage Interests owned by all Limited Partners having the right or obligation to purchase hereunder (calculated specifically excluding from the proportionate calculation the Percentage Interest subject to such purchase).

Article II
General

2.01 **Formation**. By this Agreement, the General Partner and the Limited Partners form and establish the Limited Partnership, herein called the "Partnership," under and pursuant to the Act. Prior to conducting any business in any jurisdiction, the General Partner shall execute the Certificate, and promptly cause such Certificate to be filed with the Secretary of State of the State of Texas as required by the Act and comply with all other legal requirements for the formation and operation of the Partnership. Thereafter, the General Partner shall execute and cause to be filed and otherwise published such original or amended Certificates evidencing the formation and operation of the Partnership whenever the same may be required under the laws of the State of Texas and of any other states where the Partnership shall determine to do business. No copies of Certificates of Limited Partnership, Amendment, Dissolution, or Cancellation need to be delivered to the Limited Partners. Except as expressly provided in this Agreement, the Act shall govern the rights and liabilities of the Partners.

2.02 **Name**. The name of the Partnership shall be FERGUSON FAMILY LIMITED PARTNERSHIP. The business of the Partnership may be conducted under such name or, may be conducted from time to time under different trade or fictitious names for the Partnership as it may determine appropriate, in its sole discretion as allowed under the Act.

2.03 **Investment**. Each of the Limited Partners represents that he or she is acquiring an interest in the Partnership for investment for his or her own account and not with a view to any sale or distribution of that interest.

2.04 **Merger or Conversion**. The Partnership may merge with or convert into another limited partnership or other business entity, or enter into an agreement to do so, only with the written consent of the General Partner and a Required Interest.

Article III
Commencement Date, Term of Partnership

The Partnership shall commence and be effective on the date the Certificate is filed with the Secretary of State of the State of Texas (the "Effective Date"). The Partners shall conduct no business before the Effective Date. The Partnership shall continue in existence until it is terminated, liquidated, or dissolved in accordance with this Agreement or by operation of law.

Article IV
Location of Principal Place of Business;
Registered Office and Registered Agent

The principal place of business and the mailing address of the Partnership shall be 123 Capitol Way, Austin, Texas 78701, or such other place or places as the General Partner may at any time or from time to time determine. The General Partner may establish additional places of business of the Partnership when and where required by the Partnership's business. All Partnership records required by the Act shall be maintained at the principal office. The registered office of the Partnership in the State of Texas shall be 123 Capitol Way, Austin, Texas 78701, and the registered agent of the Partnership at that address shall be James "Pa" Ferguson. The address and the name of the registered agent of the Partnership may be changed as the General Partner may designate by written notice to the Limited Partners and by filing an amended Certificate with the Secretary of State.

Article V
Purposes

The business and purpose of the Partnership shall be to engage in any or all such lawful business which may be engaged in by a limited partnership organized under the Act, as such business activities may be determined by the General Partner from time to time and to do all things necessary or incidental to the foregoing purposes. The Partnership is designed to provide a means for Family Entities to become knowledgeable of, manage, and preserve family assets. To accomplish this purpose, the Partnership may, but is not limited to, provide resolution of any disputes which arise among the Family Entities in order to preserve family harmony and avoid the expense and problems of litigation, maintain control of family assets, consolidate fractional interests in family assets, increase family wealth, establish a method by which annual gifts can be made without fractionalizing family assets, continue the ownership of family assets and restrict the right of non-Family Entities to acquire interests in family assets, provide protection to family assets from claims of future creditors against Family Entities, provide flexibility and business planning not available through other business entities, facilitate the administration and reduce the cost associated with the disability or probate of the estate of Family Entities, and promote the knowledge of and communication about family assets among Family Entities.

Article VI
Capital Contributions

6.01   Initial Partners. The initial Partners of the Partnership shall be those partners shown in the attached Exhibit A which is hereby incorporated by reference for all purposes of this Agreement.

6.02   Partnership Interests. Subject to the terms and allocation provisions of this Agreement, the Partners shall have the following percentage Partnership Interests as reflected on the attached Exhibit B which is hereby incorporated by reference for all purposes of this Agreement.

6.03   General Partner's Contribution. At the time of execution of this Agreement, in return for the Percentage Interest as set forth in Exhibit B of this Agreement, the General Partner shall contribute to the capital of the Partnership the property identified on Exhibit A attached hereto and incorporated herein by reference. Additional initial contributions by the General Partner are to be shown on an additional exhibit which may be subsequently attached to this Agreement or otherwise retained separately by the General Partner.

6.04   Limited Partners' Contributions. At the time of execution of this Agreement, in return for the Percentage Interest as set forth in Exhibit B of this Agreement, the Limited Partners shall contribute to the capital of the Partnership the property identified on Exhibit A attached hereto and incorporated herein by reference. Additional initial contributions by the Limited Partners are to be shown on an additional exhibit which may be subsequently attached to this Agreement or otherwise retained separately by the General Partner.

6.05 **Limited Liability for Limited Partners**. The liability of the Limited Partners to the Partnership is limited to the amount of their respective Capital Contributions. Accordingly, the contributions called for in Section 6.04 of this Agreement are the only property the Limited Partners are required to furnish to the Partnership, whether by way of contribution, loan, or otherwise. The Limited Partners are entitled to a return of their respective capital contribution(s) only as provided in this Agreement.

6.06 **Voluntary Contributions**. At any time, the General Partner may determine that additional contributions of cash or property to the Partnership are desirable. Within ten (10) days following the receipt of notice from the General Partner, each Limited Partner may contribute cash or property to the Partnership as a "Voluntary Capital Contribution" on the terms and subject to the conditions set forth in the notice from the General Partner. All such additional Voluntary Capital Contributions shall be requested in proportion to the then Percentage Interests of the Partners in the Partnership. However, except as otherwise provided by Texas law, the Limited Partners shall not be required to make any additional capital contributions to the Partnership in excess of their initial contributions set forth in Exhibit A.

6.07 **Readjustment of Percentage Interests**. If any Partner elects to participate in a Voluntary Capital Contribution as described in Section 6.06 of this Agreement in an amount smaller than that Partner's current Percentage Interest, or elects not to participate at all, then the Percentage Interests of the Partners shall be readjusted based on the newly adjusted capital account balance of each Partner taking into account all capital contributions that are made, including initial capital contributions. Nothing in this Agreement shall obligate any Partner to make any additional contributions to the Partnership. Notwithstanding the foregoing, the General Partner is required to maintain a Percentage Interest and capital of at least one percent (1%) at all times. Accordingly, in addition to other available means by which the General Partner would maintain a one percent (1%) Percentage Interest, the General Partner agrees to contribute capital, from time to time, in the form of cash or other property so that the General Partner maintains a Percentage Interest of no less than one percent (1%).

In the event of any adjustment to a Partner's Percentage Interest pursuant to this Section, no Partner shall have the right to modify, rectify or undo such adjustments thereafter, and such adjustments shall be made without the need for any further act, writing or consent to effect any such adjustment. Any adjustment to the Partners' respective Percentage Interests shall be set forth on an additional Exhibit to be attached hereto at the time of any and each such adjustment.

Article VII
Capital Accounts; Partnership Property

7.01   Establishment of Capital Accounts. Separate capital accounts shall be established and maintained on the books and records of the Partnership for each Partner in accordance with the Code and the Treasury Regulations, including Section 1.704-1(b) of the Treasury Regulations, as amended from time to time.

7.02   Credits and Debits. All Capital Contributions of a Partner, its allocable share of Partnership income and loss, and cash or property distributions made to such Partner shall be credited or charged to such Partner's individual capital account as the case may be. To the extent an allocation or adjustment is not specifically described by this provision of this Agreement, that item shall be reflected in the Partners' capital accounts in accordance with Section 1.704-1(b)(2)(iv) of the Treasury Regulations, as amended from time to time. The capital accounts shall not bear interest.

7.03   Accounting for Partners' Loans. Loans made by a Partner to the Partnership shall not be considered capital contributions.

7.04   Return of Capital. No Partner has the right to demand the return of its Capital Contribution other than in cash and except as provided in this Agreement.

7.05   Liquidation. When the Partnership is liquidated, each Partner with a deficit in his or her capital account (whether by virtue of loans, distribution, failure to make an initial contribution, or any other reason) will be obligated to contribute to the capital of the Partnership an amount of cash equal to the deficit in the capital account balance. The cash must be paid within one hundred eighty (180) days after the date of the liquidation, and the amounts so contributed may be paid to the creditors of the Partnership or distributed to the other Partners in the ratio of the then positive balances in their respective capital accounts.

7.06   Ownership of Partnership Property and Waiver of Right to Partition. All interests in the Partnership Property ("Property") shall be held in the name of the Partnership and shall be deemed owned by the Partnership as an entity. No Partner, individually, shall have any ownership of such Property or any interest in such Property except as a partner in the Partnership, but the interests of all Partners in the Partnership are, for all purposes, personal property. Having previously been advised that he may have a right to bring an action for partition, each of the Partners irrevocably waives, during the term of the Partnership and during any period of its liquidation following any dissolution, any right that it may have to maintain any action for partition with respect to any of the assets of the Partnership.

7.07   Legal Title to Partnership Property. Legal title to Partnership property shall be held in the name of the Partnership. Subject to the provisions of Article VIII, and the other provisions hereof, as well as their fiduciary obligations to the Limited Partners, the General Partner shall have the right, power and authority (without regard to the term of the Partnership), acting for and on behalf of the Partnership, to enter into and execute any lease, contract, agreement, deed, mortgage, or other instrument or document required or otherwise appropriate to lease, sell, mortgage, convey, refinance Partnership property (or any part thereof), to borrow money and execute promissory notes, to secure the same by mortgage (which term "mortgage" is hereby defined for all purposes of this Agreement to include deeds of trust, financing statements, chattel mortgages, pledges, conditional sales contracts, and similar security agreements) upon Partnership property, to renew or extend any and all such loans or notes, and to convey Partnership property in fee simple by deed, mortgage, or otherwise. In no event shall any party dealing with such General Partner with respect to any Partnership property, or to whom Partnership property (or any part thereof) shall be conveyed, contracted to be sold, leased, mortgaged, or refinanced (which term "refinanced" is hereby defined for all purposes of this Agreement to include recast, modified, extended, or increased) by such General Partner, be obligated to see to the application of any purchase money, rent, or money borrowed or advanced thereon, or be obligated to see that the terms of this Agreement have been complied with, or be obligated to inquire into the necessity or expediency of any act or action of such General Partner, and every contract, agreement, deed, mortgage, lease, promissory note, or other instrument or document executed by such General Partner, with respect to any Partnership property, shall be conclusive evidence in favor of any and every person relying thereon or claiming thereunder that: (a) at the time or times of the execution and/or delivery thereof, the Partnership was in full force and effect, (b) such instrument or document was duly executed and authorized and is binding upon the Partnership and all of the Partners thereof, and (c) such General Partner executing and delivering the same was duly authorized and empowered to execute and deliver any and every such instrument or document for and on behalf of the Partnership. It is expressly understood and agreed that the manner of holding title to Partnership property (or any part thereof) and any Partnership assets are solely for the convenience of the Partnership. Accordingly, the spouse, heirs, executors or administrators, beneficiaries, distributees, successors, or assigns, of any Partner shall have no right, title or interest in or to any Partnership property or Partnership assets regardless of the manner in which title is held; rather, Partnership property and any Partnership assets shall be subject to the terms of this Agreement.

Article VIII
Control and Management

8.01   General Partner's Authority. Subject to the consent of the Partners where required by this Agreement, the Partnership shall be managed by the General Partner. Unless otherwise set forth herein, all decisions relating to the business and affairs of the Partnership including, without limitation, all decisions required or permitted to be made by the General Partner under this Agreement and all decisions required or permitted to be made by the Partnership as a participant in any other legal entity in which it may have an interest, may be made and any necessary action taken by the General Partner. In making such decisions, the General Partner shall exercise ordinary, prudent business judgment. All such decisions by the General Partner hereunder shall be binding upon all of the Partners and the Partnership. All approvals and/or consents or actions required by the Partners herein may be prospective or retroactive, unless otherwise specifically provided hereby.

8.02   Specific Power and Authority of General Partner. Unless otherwise set forth herein, the power and authority of the General Partner to make all decisions with respect to the business and affairs of the Partnership and, so far as dealings with third parties are concerned, the power and authority of the General Partner to take such action for and on behalf of the Partnership as it may deem necessary or appropriate to enable the Partnership to carry out its purposes as set forth herein, shall include, without limitation, the power and authority:

141

(a)   To acquire in any manner, either directly or indirectly, through ownership interests or other participation by other entities, such real property, tangible personal property and intangible personal property as may be necessary or desirable to carry on the business of the Partnership and to sell, lease, exchange, or otherwise dispose of such property.

(b)   To delegate all or any of its duties under this Agreement and in furtherance of any such delegation may appoint, employ, or contract with any person that it, in its sole discretion, deems necessary or desirable for the transaction of the business of the Partnership, which person may, under the supervision of the General Partner: (i) administer the day-to-day operations of the Partnership; (ii) serve as the Partnership's advisors and consultants in connection with policy and investment decisions made by the General Partner; (iii) act as consultants, accountants, correspondents, attorneys, brokers, escrow agents, or in any other capacity deemed by the General Partner to be necessary or desirable; (iv) investigate, select, and, on behalf of the Partnership, conduct relations with persons acting in those capacities and pay appropriate fees to, and enter into appropriate contracts with, or employ, or retain services performed or to be performed by, any of them in connection with the business of the Partnership; (v) perform or assist in the performance of those administrative or managerial functions necessary in the management of the Partnership as may be agreed upon with the General Partner; and (vi) perform such other acts or services for the Partnership as the General Partner, in its sole and absolute discretion and in accordance with the provisions of this Agreement may approve;

(c)   To execute, sign, and deliver in furtherance of any or all of the purposes of the Partnership, any and all agreements, contracts, documents, certifications, subscriptions, and other instruments necessary or convenient in connection with the business of the Partnership all of which may contain such terms, provisions, and conditions as the General Partner, in its sole and absolute discretion, shall deem appropriate and to do any and all other acts or things necessary, proper, convenient, or advisable to effectuate and carry out the intent and purposes of the Partnership;

(d)   To institute, prosecute, defend and settle any legal, arbitration or administrative actions or proceedings on behalf of or against the Partnership;

(e)   To exercise any and all rights of a shareholder or holder of any interest held by the Partnership, including, but not limited to, voting such interest in the sole and absolute discretion of the General Partner;

(f)   To maintain and operate the assets of the Partnership or any part or parts thereof;

(g)   To pay any debts and other obligations of the Partnership, including amounts due under permanent financing of improvements and other loans to the Partnership and costs of operation and maintenance of the assets of the Partnership;

(h)   To require in any Partnership contracts that the General Partner shall not have any personal liability thereon but that the person or entity contracting with the Partnership is to look solely to the Partnership and its assets for satisfaction;

(i)   To cause the Partnership to make or revoke any of the elections under the Code or any other taxing authority that is made at the Partnership level;

(j)   To deposit all monies received for or on behalf of the Partnership in appropriate banking or investment accounts and to disburse and pay all funds on deposit on behalf of the Partnership in such amounts and at such times as the same are required in connection with the ownership, maintenance and operation of the assets of the Partnership;

(k)   To prepare, or have prepared, and file all tax returns for the Partnership (but not the tax returns or other reporting of the individual Partners, or of their respective heirs, representatives, executors or assigns, in their individual capacities);

(l)   To perform other obligations provided elsewhere in this Agreement to be performed by the General Partner, unless this Agreement specifically requires action by other Partners;

(m)   To borrow money and issue evidences of indebtedness, and to secure the same by mortgage, deed of trust, pledge, security interest, encumbrance, or other lien on any assets of the Partnership, real or personal, in connection with transactions necessary, convenient or incidental to the accomplishment of the purposes of the Partnership;

(n)   To make appropriate short term investments, pending application of the Partners' Capital Contributions to investments, as deemed advisable by the General Partner, in order to utilize any cash on hand not then required for working capital or the immediate payment of the Partnership obligations; and

(o)   To engage in any kind of activity and to perform and carry out contracts of any kind necessary to, or in connection with, or incidental to the accomplishment of the purposes of the Partnership as may be lawfully carried on or performed by a Partnership under the laws of each state in which the Partnership is then formed or qualified.

8.03   Limited Powers of General Partner.

(a)   Notwithstanding the generality of the General Partner's authority, the General Partner is not empowered, without the written consent of a Required Interest of the Limited Partners, to:

(i)   Terminate, liquidate, and wind up the Partnership, except as otherwise provided in Article XIII;

(ii)   Admit additional or substitute General Partners except as provided in Articles XII and XIII;

(iii)   Do any act that would make it impossible to carry out the ordinary business of the Partnership, except as specifically permitted by the terms of this Agreement;

(iv)   Prior to the actual termination of the Partnership, sell substantially all of the Property in liquidation or cessation of business;

(v)   Possess Partnership Property or assign any rights in specific Partnership Property for other than a Partnership purpose;

(vi)   Require any Partner to make any contribution to the capital of the Partnership not provided for in this Agreement;

(vii)   Engage in any business activity inconsistent with the purpose of the Partnership (which, it is recognized, is unlimited other than as limited by law);

(viii)   Amend this Agreement except as provided for elsewhere in this Agreement; or

(ix)   Do any other act in contravention of this Agreement.

(b)   Notwithstanding anything to the contrary in Section 8.03(a), should there be exactly two (2) Limited Partners each owing an equal Percentage Interest, then, in that event, if only one of the Limited Partners plus the General Partner consent in writing to the General Partner's authority to take the actions enumerated in Section 8.03(a), then the General Partner shall be authorized to take such action without the consent of the other Limited Partner.

8.04   Reliance By Third Parties Upon General Partner's Statement.   Any person dealing with the Partnership, other than a Partner, may rely on the authority of the General Partner in taking any action in the name of the Partnership without inquiry into the provisions of this Agreement.   Any Statement signed by the General Partner shall be deemed to be the action of the Partnership as to third parties.   Any person dealing with the Partnership or the General Partner may rely upon a written Statement signed by the General Partner as to:

(a)   The identity of any Partner;

(b)   Any conditions precedent to acts by the Partnership;

(c)   The Persons who are authorized to execute and deliver any instrument or document of the Partnership and bind the Partnership;

(d)   Any act or failure to act by the Partnership or as to any other matter whatsoever involving the Partnership or any Partner when such Statement is made in accordance with section 8.04 of this Agreement.

After delivering such Statement, the General Partner, by the General Partner's signature alone, may sign any instrument and bind the Partnership and the Partnership Property.   Such Statement shall not, however, be determinative as between the Partners unless the action in question was in fact authorized or permitted in accordance with this Agreement.

8.05 **Other and Competing Activities.** Unless provided otherwise in any employment contracts between the Partnership and any Partners ("Employment Contract"), any Partner may engage in or possess an interest in other business ventures of any nature or description, independently or with others, similar to or competitive with the business conducted by the Partnership with no obligation to offer the Partnership or any other Partner the right to participate. If not prohibited by an Employment Contract, neither the Partnership nor any Partner, other than the Partner participating in the activity or possessing the competing interest, shall have any rights in or to such independent ventures or to the income or profits derived from these other activities.

8.06 **Liability of General Partner.** The General Partner is not liable, responsible, or accountable in damages or otherwise to the Limited Partners or the Partnership for any act performed by the General Partner in good faith and within the scope of this Agreement. The General Partner is liable to the Limited Partners and the Partnership only for acts or omissions that involve bad faith, misconduct, or fraud.

8.07 **Indemnification of General Partner.** The Partnership shall indemnify and hold harmless the General Partner and its officers, directors, agents, and representatives from and against any loss, damage, liability, cost or expense (including reasonable attorneys' fees) arising out of any act or failure to act by the General Partner when such act or omission is made by the General Partner in good faith and within the scope of this Agreement, specifically including its sole, partial, or concurrent negligence, to the greatest extent permitted under the Act.

8.08 **Contracts with Affiliates.** Notwithstanding anything in this Agreement to the contrary, it is understood and agreed that the Partnership may employ any Partner and any person affiliated with any Partner to render services on behalf of the Partnership and may compensate the person rendering the services on customary terms and at competitive rates. Neither the Partnership nor the other Partners shall have any rights in or to any profits derived from any fees paid by the Partnership for such services.

8.09 **Tax Matters Partner.** The General Partner is authorized and required to represent the Partnership in connection with all examinations of the Partnership affairs by tax authorities, including administrative and judicial proceedings, and to expend Partnership funds for professional services and costs in connection with such examinations. The General Partner is the "Tax Matters Partner" for federal tax purposes and has authority, in its sole and absolute discretion, to represent the Partnership and the Partners in this regard. The Limited Partners agree to cooperate and to do or refrain from doing any and all things reasonably required by the Tax Matters Partner to conduct these sorts of proceedings.

8.10 **Compensation of General Partner.** The General Partner shall be entitled to reimbursement for any expenses that it advances for Partnership business. In addition, the General Partner may receive reasonable annual compensation for services rendered to the Partnership. Reasonable compensation is to be measured by the time required in the administration of the Partnership, the responsibilities assumed in the discharge of such administration, and the value of Property under the General Partner's administration.

Article IX
Rights and Obligations of Limited Partners

9.01 **Limited Liability.** The Limited Partners have no personal liability whatsoever, whether to the Partnership, the General Partner, or any creditor of the Partnership, for any of the debts or losses of the Partnership beyond their respective Capital Contributions to the Partnership.

9.02 **Return of Distributions.** In accordance with state law, a limited partner of a partnership may, under certain circumstances, be required to return to the partnership, for the benefit of partnership creditors, amounts previously distributed to that partner as a result of a return of capital. It is the intent of the Partners that no distribution of cash to any Limited Partner shall be deemed a return or withdrawal of capital (even if that distribution is treated, in whole or in part, for any purpose as a distribution out of a reserve for depreciation or other reserve which is attributable to depreciation or any other non-cash item accounted for as a loss or deduction from or offset to the Partnership's income), and that no Limited Partner shall be obligated to pay any such amount to or for the account of the Partnership or any creditor of the Partnership. However, if any court of competent jurisdiction holds that, notwithstanding the provisions of this Agreement, a Limited Partner is obligated to make any such payment, that obligation shall be the obligation of that Limited Partner and not of the General Partner.

9.03 **Limited Partners' Authority to Act.** The Limited Partners shall not take part in the management or control of the business, transact any business of the Partnership, or have the power to sign for or to bind the Partnership. This provision shall not, however, prevent a Limited Partner from:

      (a)   Acting in a capacity or exercising a power irrevocably granted to a Limited Partner under the Act; or

      (b)   Acting in a capacity or exercising a power of a Limited Partner granted under this Agreement if and when such action or power is specifically enumerated in Section 3.03(b) of the Act.

No Limited Partner shall be granted any authority inconsistent with the provisions of the Act and to the extent any provision in this Agreement grants authority to a Limited Partner in excess of that deemed appropriate under the Act, such provision shall be deemed invalid and severed from this Agreement in accordance with Section 21.05 of this Agreement.

9.04 **Voting of Limited Partners.** The Limited Partners shall have the right to vote upon the matters listed below:

      (a)   Election of a successor General Partner;

      (b)   Removal of the General Partner;

      (c)   Admission of an additional General Partner;

      (d)   Termination and dissolution of the Partnership;

(e)   Amendment of this Agreement;

(f)   The extension of the term of the Partnership;

(g)   Transfer or assignment of an interest in the Partnership; and

(h)   Any matter requiring the vote of the Limited Partners as set out elsewhere in this Agreement or in the Act.

All votes by the Limited Partners, unless otherwise provided by the Act, shall be determined by the vote of the Required Interest, which Required Interest vote shall be determinative and binding on all of the Limited Partners. Those matters to be voted on by the Limited Partners may be done by written consent. Such a written consent may be utilized at any meeting of the Partners, or it may be utilized in obtaining approval by the Partners without a meeting.

Article X
Percentage Interests; Allocations and Distributions

10.01   Accounting Principles. The net income and net loss of the Partnership (and each item of income, gain, loss, deduction, or credit entering into the computation of net income and net loss) shall be determined on an annual basis in accordance with the accounting methods followed by the Partnership for federal income tax purposes and otherwise in accordance with generally accepted accounting principles and procedures.

10.02   Percentage Interests.

(a) The initial Percentage Interest of each Partner shall be as set forth in Exhibit B attached to this Agreement.

(b) The Percentage Interest of each Partner may be adjusted from time to time by the methods and for the reasons described elsewhere in this Agreement including, but not limited to, the provisions of Sections 6.06 and 6.07 of this Agreement.

10.03   Allocations. All net income, net losses, and credits and items of gain or loss of the Partnership shall be allocated to each Partner in accordance with each Partner's Percentage Interest.

10.04   Distributions. All cash flow available for distribution to the Partners, subject to the establishment of reserves in the General Partner's reasonable determination, shall be distributed to the Partners in accordance with their respective Percentage Interests, unless otherwise unanimously agreed to by the Partners.

10.05   Compliance with Treasury Regulations. It is intended that the allocation and distribution provisions set forth in this Article X apply in a manner consistent with the provisions of Section 704 and 706 of the Code, and the Treasury Regulations promulgated for those Sections. The General Partner shall have reasonable discretion to apply the allocation and distribution provisions set forth in this Article X in any manner consistent with Sections 704 and 706 of the Code and the Treasury Regulations.

Article XI
Loans to Partnership

Pursuant to a written agreement approved by the General Partner, any Partner may lend funds to the Partnership for Partnership business. Loans made under this provision of this Agreement shall be deemed an obligation of indebtedness from the Partnership to the Partner, payable prior to any distributions to the Partners.

Article XII
Transfers of Partnership Interests; Additional Partnership Interests

12.01 Restriction on Transfers by Limited Partners. Except as specifically enumerated in this Article XII of this Agreement, no Limited Partner may sell, transfer, assign, mortgage, hypothecate or otherwise encumber or permit or suffer any encumbrance of all or any portion of his or its interest in the Partnership without the prior written consent of a Required Interest. Any Limited Partner may grant or withhold consent, even arbitrarily, in his sole and absolute discretion. Any attempt to transfer or encumber any such interest in the Partnership, except as specifically provided for and allowed under this Article XII, shall be null and void, ab initio, and of no force or effect.

12.02 Permitted Assignees/Transferees. Notwithstanding anything to the contrary in this Agreement, a Limited Partner may transfer or dispose of all or any part of his Percentage Interest by gift or by sale to another Partner, to a member or members of the transferor's Immediate Family or to a trust for the primary benefit of some or all of the transferor's Immediate Family or to a trust for the benefit of a spouse which is "qualified terminable interest property" as described in Section 2056 of the Code, provided the Partnership interest held by the trust will be distributed to a member or members of the Immediate Family on the death of the spouse (collectively "Permitted Transferee"). If a trust is a Partner, the trustee may distribute or sell the Partnership interest held by the trust to trust beneficiary who is a member of the Immediate Family or to any Partner.

12.03 Transfer of Partnership Interest by Sale. No Permitted Transferee of all or part of the interest of the Limited Partners in the Partnership shall have the right to become a substitute Limited Partner unless all of the following occur:

(a) The transferring Limited Partner has stated the intention that the Permitted Transferee become a Limited Partner in his or her own right in the instrument of assignment;

(b) The Permitted Transferee has executed an instrument, the terms of which do not contravene any of the provisions of this Agreement, witnessing the Permitted Transferee's acceptance and adoption of the terms and provisions of this Agreement and affirmatively agreeing to be bound by the terms hereof, including executing a joinder to this Agreement in substantially the same form as Exhibit C attached hereto;

(c)   The assignment or transfer is received by the Partnership and recorded in the books of the Partnership; and

(d)   The transferring Limited Partner or assignee pays any reasonable expenses in connection with the admission of the assignee as a Limited Partner.

12.04   Transfer of Partnership Interest by Death or Gift. Upon the death of any Partner, his Partnership Interest may pass by will or intestacy to any existing Partner, the Immediate Family of any Partner, or a trust as set out in Section 12.02. However, the Partnership Interest passing to such legatees or donees shall be subject to the terms of this Agreement in the hands of such legatee or donee. Such legatee and donee shall execute a joinder to this Agreement in substantially the same form as Exhibit C attached hereto. If a Partnership interest will pass to someone other than an existing Partner, the Immediate Family of a deceased Partner, or a trust described in Section 12.02, the Partner making a gift or bequest of a Partnership Interest (the "Donor") or the estate of the deceased Partner shall give written notice to the Partnership and the other Partners, which notice shall:

(a)   State that the deceased Partner has died or the Donor intends to make a gift or bequest;

(b)   Identify the legatee or donee (a copy of the trust agreement shall accompany the notice if the legatee or done is a trust); and

(c)   State the percentage of Partnership Interest bequeathed or to be gifted.

The written notice shall be given by the Administrator or Executor of the estate of the deceased Partner or the Donor to the Partners, the Immediate Family of such deceased Partner or Donor, and the Partnership within thirty (30) days after the qualification of such Administrator or Executor of the estate of the deceased Partner or prior to making the gift or bequest.

For sixty (60) days after the giving of such notice, the existing Partners in the Immediate Family of the deceased Partner or Donor shall have the option to purchase the Partnership Interest which is set forth in the notice. Each Partner in the deceased Partner's Immediate Family (including any trust) desiring to purchase a portion of the Partnership Interest shall be entitled to purchase an amount of Partnership Interest proportional to that Purchasing Partner's Partnership Interest among the entire Partnership Interest as determined at the time of notification of Partner's desire to purchase. A Partner desiring to purchase shall exercise his option by a signed written notice to the Executor or Administrator of the estate of the deceased Partner or the Donor within the sixty- (60-) day option period.

If the offer is rejected in whole or in part by the Partners in the Immediate Family of the deceased Partner or Donor during the initial sixty- (60-) day option period or during the Back Out Period (hereafter defined) provided in Section 12.05(b), or if no person in the Immediate Family is a Partner, the other Partners shall have the option to purchase the remaining Partnership Interest for a period of forty-five (45) days following the expiration of the later of the option period in which the Partners in the Immediate Family of the deceased Partner or Donor could elect to purchase or the Back Out Period. Each other Partner shall have an option to purchase a percentage of the offered

Partnership Interest (or the portion thereof not purchased by the Partners in the Immediate Family of the deceased Partner or Donor) which is proportional to its Partnership Interest as compared with the Partnership Interests of other Purchasing Partners. The other Partners together with the Partners in the Immediate Family of the deceased Partner or Donor must elect to purchase all, and not less than all, of the Partnership Interest subject to the option. A Partner desiring to purchase shall exercise the option by a signed written notice to the Executor or Administrator of the estate of the deceased Partner or the Donor within the option period.

If, at the expiration of the option period and the Back Out Period, the other Partners and the Partners in the Immediate Family of the deceased Partner have not exercised the option and elected to purchase all, and not less than all, of the deceased Partner's Partnership Interest subject to the option, the Estate of the deceased Partner may hold such Partnership Interest and distribute it as provided by the Will of the deceased Partner, or by intestacy if there is no Will, but the Partnership interest in the hands of the recipient shall be subject to the terms of this Agreement. Such recipient shall execute a joinder to this Agreement in substantially the same form as Exhibit C attached hereto. If, at the expiration of the option period and Back Out Period, the other Partners and the Partners in the Immediate Family of the Donor have not exercised the option and elected to purchase all, and not less than all, of the Donor's Partnership Interest subject to the option, the Donor can make the gift, but the Partnership Interest in the hands of the recipient shall be subject to the terms of this Agreement.

12.05 Purchase Price for Transfer. The purchase price for purposes of Section 12.04 shall be determined as follows:

(a) The Executor or other personal representative of the Estate of the deceased Partner, or the Donor, and the General Partner shall agree on an appraiser who shall appraise the Partnership Interest which is subject to this option at fair market value as of the date of the deceased Partner's death or the date of the proposed gift, taking into account in determining the fair market value of such Partnership Interest any appropriate discounts for lack of marketability, lack of control, and any other factors affecting the fair market value of the Partnership Interest being appraised. The appraisal shall be made only after the option to purchase under this Section 12.05 has been exercised. The appraised value of such Partnership Interest shall constitute the purchase price for purposes of this Section 12.05.

(b) For a period of sixty (60) days following the date upon which the completed appraisal is submitted to the persons exercising the option, the person or persons exercising the option to purchase may elect not to purchase the deceased Partner or Donor's Partnership Interest by submitting such decision in writing to the Executor or Administrator of the Estate of the Deceased Partner or to the Donor. This sixty- (60-) day period shall be referred to as the "Back Out Period." If for any reason during or after the Back Out Period the Partners who have exercised the option fail to purchase the Partnership Interest, such Partners shall pay for the entire cost of the appraisal. If the Partners who have exercised the option fail to purchase, another written notice shall be given by the estate of the deceased Partner or the Donor as required by subsection (a) of Section 12.04, and the options set forth in Section 12.04 shall again exist except that the Partners who had previously exercised the option but failed to purchase shall not have any further option.

150

(c)   If the Partners who exercise the option do in fact purchase the Partnership Interest, the cost of such appraisal shall be paid equally by the Estate of the deceased Partner or the Donor and the Partnership.

(d)   If the personal representative of a deceased Partner, or the Donor, and the General Partners cannot agree on an appraiser, the personal representative of the deceased Partner or the Donor shall select an appraiser (and bear the cost thereof) and the General Partners shall select an appraiser (whose cost shall be paid by the Partnership). The two appraisers shall select a third appraiser (whose cost shall be paid equally by the Estate or Donor and the Partnership), and the three appraisers by majority vote will appraise the Partnership Interest as provided in this Section 12.05(a). If the Partners during the Back Out Period elect not to purchase such Partnership Interest, the cost of all appraisals shall be borne by the Partners that fail to purchase the optioned Partnership Interest.

(e)   Unless otherwise agreed by the parties, twenty-five percent (25%) of the sale price shall be paid in cash at closing. The remaining seventy-five percent (75%) of the sale price, together with interest at an annual rate determined at closing to be the applicable federal mid-term rate for the month of the closing as set forth in Section 1274(d) of the Code shall be amortized in five (5) equal annual installments of principal, the first due and payable one (1) year from the date of closing. Accrued interest on the remaining balance shall be paid with each payment of principal. The purchaser shall execute a promissory note evidencing said debt at closing, and shall have the right to prepay principal and accrued interest without penalty. Upon default in the timely payment of any installment or the insolvency or bankruptcy of the purchaser, the entire unpaid balance of the promissory note, plus all interest accrued to the date of said default, shall become due and payable, at the option of the holder thereof, and the purchaser shall pay to such representative or successor in interest all costs and expenses, including attorney's fees, incurred by the holder as a result of said default or in collecting said note.

(f)   Any sale under this Agreement shall be closed at the principal office of the Partnership during normal business hours on a date, mutually agreeable to all parties, which is not more than thirty (30) days after the expiration of the option period.

12.06   Disclosures, Limitations, and Exceptions.   The ownership and transfer or assignment of an interest in the Partnership is further subject to the following disclosures, limitations and exceptions:

(a)   *Federal Law Disclosure and Limitations.* Each Partner is aware, as disclosed in Section 20.02 of this Agreement, that the interests in the Partnership have not, nor will be, registered under federal or state securities laws. Interests in the Partnership may not be offered for sale, sold, pledged, or otherwise transferred unless so registered, or unless an exemption from registration exists. The availability of any exemption from registration must be established by an opinion of counsel, whose opinion must be satisfactory to the General Partner.

(b)   *Nonrecognition of an Unauthorized Transfer.* The Partnership will not be required to recognize the interest of any assignee or transferee who has obtained a purported interest in the Partnership as the result of a transfer or assignment which is not authorized by this Agreement. If there is a doubt as to ownership of an interest in the Partnership or as to who is entitled to a cash distribution or liquidating proceeds or other Property, the General Partner may accumulate cash or liquidation proceeds or other Property as to the ownership interest that is in doubt until the issue is resolved to the satisfaction of the General Partner.

(c)   *Acquisition of an Interest Conveyed to Another Without Authority.* If any Person acquires an interest in the Partnership, or becomes an assignee, as the result of an order of a court which the Partnership is required by law to recognize, or if a Partner's interest in the Partnership is subjected to a lawful "charging order," or if a Partner makes an unauthorized transfer or assignment of an interest in the Partnership, which the Partnership is required by law (and by order of a court) to recognize, the Partnership will have the unilateral option to acquire the interest of the transferee or assignee, or any fraction or part thereof, upon the following terms and conditions:

(i)   The Partnership will have the option to acquire the interest by giving written notice to the transferee or assignee of its intent to purchase within ninety (90) days from the date that the Partnership receives notice that it has finally been determined, if at all, that the Partnership is required to recognize the transfer or assignment.

(ii)   The valuation date for the determination of the purchase price of the interest will be the first day of the month following the month in which notice is delivered.

(iii)   Unless the Partnership and the transferee or assignee agree otherwise, the purchase price for the interest, or any fraction to be acquired by the Partnership, shall be its fair market value as determined by an appraisal commissioned by the Partnership, as provided for in Section 12.05 of this Agreement.

(iv)   Closing of the sale will occur at the principal office of the Partnership at 10 o'clock a.m. on the first Tuesday of the month following the month in which the appraisal is rendered.

(v)   In order to reduce the burden upon the resources of the Partnership, the Partnership will have the option, to be exercised in writing delivered at closing, to pay its purchase money obligation in fifteen (15) equal annual principal installments (or the remaining term of the Partnership if less than fifteen (15) years) plus interest on all outstanding principal at a rate per annum equal from time to time until the purchase price (plus interest) is paid in full to the lesser of (1) the Wall Street Journal prime rate as quoted in the money rate section of the Wall Street Journal or (2) the maximum rate permitted by applicable law. The first installment of principal, with interest, will be due and payable on the tenth (10th) day of the calendar year following closing, and subsequent annual installments, with accrued interest, will be due and payable on the tenth day of each succeeding calendar year until the entire amount of the obligation is paid. The Partnership will have the right to prepay all or any part of the purchase money obligation at any time without penalty or premium.

(vi)   By consent of a Required Interest, calculated without inclusion of the Partner whose interest is to be acquired, the General Partner may assign the Partnership's option to purchase to one or more of the remaining Partners and, when done, any rights or obligations imposed upon the Partnership will instead become, by substitution, the rights and obligations of the Partners who are assignees.

(vii)   Neither the transferee nor assignee of an unauthorized transfer or assignment or the Partner causing the transfer or assignment will have the right to vote on Partnership matters during the prescribed option period or, if the option to purchase is timely exercised, until the sale is closed.

12.07   General Partner as Limited Partner. If the General Partner should acquire an interest as a Limited Partner, the General Partner shall, with respect to such interest, enjoy all the rights and be subject to all the obligations and duties of a Limited Partner to the extent of such interest.

12.08   Transfer by General Partner. The General Partner may not transfer any or all of its interest in the Partnership without the prior written consent of a Required Interest. If a transfer is approved, the transferee assumes all of the obligations of the General Partner and the General Partner shall be relieved of all further obligations and responsibilities. If a transfer of the General Partner's interest is approved, the transfer will not cause the dissolution of the Partnership, which may continue with the transferee as the General Partner the same as if the transferee had been the initial General Partner. Upon the substitution of a new General Partner, the Partnership shall cause the Certificate to be amended with the Secretary of State as required by the Act.

The restrictions on the transfer of the General Partner's interest in the Partnership shall not apply to a transfer by the General Partner to an Affiliate of the General Partner.

12.09   Admission of Additional Partners. The initial Partners are those persons who executed this Agreement as General or Limited Partners as of the Effective Date. After the Effective Date, no person shall be admitted as an additional Partner except as provided in this Agreement and the Act. In addition to any and all other prerequisites as otherwise provided by this Agreement, any additional Partner must accept and assume the terms and conditions of this Agreement in writing as a precondition to becoming a Partner by executing a joinder to this Agreement in substantially the same form as Exhibit C attached hereto. A person who is admitted as a Partner shall have the rights and obligations of a Limited Partner or General Partner as applicable. Upon the admission of an additional Partner or Partners, the Partnership shall amend this Agreement by attaching an exhibit reflecting the name(s), capital contribution, and Percentage Interest of all Partners including the additional Partner(s) as of the date of the amendment.

12.10   Admission of Additional General Partner(s). Additional General Partners may acquire an interest in the Partnership only with the prior written consent of a Required Interest. Upon the admission of an additional General Partner, the Partnership shall cause the Certificate to be amended with the Secretary of State as required by the Act.

12.11   Admission of Additional Limited Partner(s). Additional Limited Partners may acquire an interest in the Partnership only with the prior written consent of a Required Interest.

12.12   Non-Waiver of Rights. The purchase rights granted to the Partnership and the Partners by this Article XII may be exercised by the Partnership and the Partners from time to time upon the occurrence of any of the events of purchase enumerated in this Agreement, and an election by the Partnership or a Partner not to purchase on any one occasion, shall not prejudice its or his or their rights to elect to purchase on a later occasion of the happening of the same, similar or different occurrence giving rise to the right to make such purchase.

Article XIII
Dissolution and Termination

13.01 Events of Dissolution. The Partnership shall be dissolved and its business wound up on the earliest occurrence of any one of the following events:

(a) The expiration of the term of the Partnership as set forth in Article III, if any.

(b) The General Partner's determination, with the prior written consent of a Required Interest, that the Partnership should be dissolved.

(c) The dissolution, withdrawal, or bankruptcy of the General Partner, unless the Partnership is reconstituted in the manner prescribed in Section 13.02 of this Agreement. The dissolution, withdrawal, or bankruptcy of the General Partner will not result in the dissolution of the Partnership so long as the successor to the General Partner's interest in the Partnership, in accordance with Section 13.02 of this Agreement, assumes all of the General Partner's obligations under this Agreement.

13.02 Election of New General Partner. At the time of the withdrawal, dissolution, or bankruptcy of the General Partner, the business of the Partnership shall be continued on the terms and subject to the conditions of this Agreement if, within ninety (90) days after such event, the Limited Partners unanimously elect that the business of the Partnership should be continued and, in such election, by unanimous written consent, designate one or more persons to be substituted as General Partner. Any new General Partner(s) elected by this procedure will succeed to all of the powers, privileges, and obligations of the then-existing General Partner. The interest in the Partnership of the General Partner who is succeeded by any new General Partner(s) will become a Limited Partner's interest in the Partnership. In the event of the dissolution, withdrawal, or bankruptcy of the General Partner and the failure of the Limited Partners to elect to continue the business of the Partnership, the Partnership shall be terminated forthwith. Upon the substitution of a new General Partner, the Partnership shall cause the Certificate to be amended with the Secretary of State as required by the Act.

13.03 No Release From Liabilities. It is understood and agreed that no dissolution of the Partnership releases or relieves any of the parties to this Agreement of their contractual obligations under this Agreement.

13.04 Distributions in Liquidation. If the business of the Partnership is not continued, the General Partner shall, if possible, act as liquidator. If the General Partner has itself dissolved, withdrawn from the Partnership, or declared or suffered a bankruptcy, and if the Partnership is not reconstituted with a new General Partner as provided in this Agreement, a Limited Partner shall act as liquidator. The liquidator shall liquidate the assets of the Partnership, make appropriate adjustments to the capital accounts of the Partners, and distribute the proceeds in the following order of priorities, so far as the proceeds will go:

(a)   To the payment of debts of the Partnership (other than loans made from the Partners to the Partnership), including the expenses of liquidation and any state and/or federal taxes currently owed or accrued through the time of dissolution.

(b)   To the repayment of any loans that have been made by the Partners to the Partnership, but if the amount available for such repayment is insufficient, then pro rata up to the amounts available.

(c)   To all Partners pro rata in accordance with their respective capital account balances, as adjusted, up to the amounts of those capital accounts.

(d)   To all Partners pro rata according to their respective Percentage Interests in the Partnership.

13.05   Distributions In Kind. In the event any or all of the assets of the Partnership cannot be liquidated, those assets are to be distributed in kind according to the priorities set forth in Section 13.04 of this Agreement. Assets of the Partnership distributed to the Partners shall be held and owned by the Partners as tenants in common. In the event of the distribution of Partnership Properties in kind, the fair market value of such assets shall be determined by agreement of the Partners. The amount of gain or loss which would have been realized by the Partnership for federal income tax purposes if the assets had been sold at such fair market value rather than distributed in kind shall be treated as gain or loss from a disposition of the assets of the Partnership, and allocated among the Partners in accordance with Article X, such allocations then being reflected in the Partners' respective capital accounts.

13.06   Waiver of Right to Decree of Dissolution. The parties hereby agree that irreparable damage would be done to the goodwill and reputation of the Partnership if any Partner should bring an action in court to dissolve the Partnership. Care has been taken in this Agreement to provide what the parties have determined is fair and just payment in liquidation of the interest of all Partners. Accordingly, each party hereby waives and renounces any rights to a court decree of dissolution or to seek the appointment by the court of a liquidator for the Partnership.

Article XIV
Accounting

14.01   Fiscal Year. The fiscal year of the Partnership shall begin on the 1st day of January of each year and end on the 31st day of December of each year.

14.02   Books and Records. The General Partner shall keep at the principal place of business, or cause to be kept, full and accurate records of all transactions of the Partnership in accordance with principles and practices generally accepted for the cash or accrual method of accounting.

14.03   Inspection of Records. Any Partner may, for any proper purpose during regular business hours, inspect and copy any of the Partnership books and records at the principal place of business of the Partnership as provided in Article IV, or make other reasonable inquiries as to the

Partnership affairs. Costs of reproducing or copying Partnership books and records shall be at the expense of the Partnership.

    14.04 Tax Returns. The General Partner shall prepare and timely file all federal, state, and local tax returns required to be filed by the Partnership and, in connection with those tax returns, make any available or necessary elections. The General Partner shall deliver a copy of each such return to the Partners for review on or before ten (10) days prior to the due date (including extensions) of any such return. The Partnership shall bear the costs of the preparation and filing of the Partnership's returns.

Article XV
Reports and Statements

    Within one hundred twenty (120) days after the end of each fiscal year of the Partnership, the General Partner will deliver to the Limited Partners, at the Partnership's expense, financial statements setting forth, as of the end of and for that fiscal year, the following:

    (a)   A profit and loss statement and a balance sheet of the Partnership;

    (b)   The balance in the capital account of each Partner; and

    (c)   Any other information that, in the judgment of the General Partner, is reasonably necessary for the Limited Partner to be advised of the results of operations of the Partnership.

Article XVI
Bank Accounts

    The General Partner shall open and maintain a special bank account or accounts in which all funds of the Partnership shall be deposited. Withdrawals from such account or accounts may be made on the signature or signatures of those persons designated by the General Partner.

    The General Partner may not commingle the assets of the Partnership with the assets of any other entity or person. However, the revenues and other receipts of the Partnership may be deposited in a central account in the name of the General Partner or an affiliate of the General Partner, so long as separate entries are made on the books and records of the affiliate reflecting deposits in the bank account of the affiliate with respect to amounts received from the Partnership and withdrawals from the bank accounts made for the purpose of disbursing funds to the Partnership or for the purpose of paying liabilities of the Partnership.

Article XVII
Notices

    Whenever any notice is required or permitted to be given under this Agreement, the notice must be in writing and signed by or on behalf of the person giving the notice. The notice will be deemed to have been given when delivered by personal delivery or deposited in the United States mail, postage prepaid, certified mail, return receipt requested, properly addressed to the persons who must receive notice at the addresses listed in this Agreement or as changed by written notice given according to this provision of this Agreement.

Article XVIII
Power of Attorney

The Limited Partners irrevocably appoint the General Partner, its successors and assigns, as their respective true and lawful attorney-in-fact, with full power and authority, on their behalf and in their respective names, to execute, acknowledge, swear to, deliver and, if appropriate, file in such offices and places as may be required by law (i) any amendment to this Agreement that may be required by a change in the name of the Partnership, change in registered agent, or similar matter; and (ii) any amendment to this Agreement made in compliance with Article XIX. The power of attorney granted by the Limited Partners to the General Partner is a special power coupled with an interest and is irrevocable, and may be exercised by any party who, at the time of exercise, is a General Partner of the Partnership. The power of attorney shall survive any transfer or abandonment of a Limited Partner's interest in the Partnership, or the Limited Partner's withdrawal from the Partnership.

Article XIX
Amendment

This Agreement may be amended or modified by written instrument executed by both the General Partner and a Required Interest.

Article XX
Investment and Other Representations
of the Partners

20.01 **Investment Intent**. Each of the Partners does hereby represent and warrant to the Partnership and to each other Partner that he or she has acquired his or her interest in the Partnership for investment, solely for his or her own account, with the intention of holding such interest in the Partnership for investment, and without any intention of participating directly or indirectly in any redistribution or resale of any portion of such interest in violation of the Securities Act of 1933, as amended (the "Securities Act") or any applicable state securities law.

20.02 **Unregistered Partnership Interests**. Each of the Partners does hereby acknowledge that he or she is aware that his or her interest in the Partnership has not been registered under the Securities Act in reliance upon exemptions contained in such Securities Act and that his or her interest in the Partnership has not been registered under the securities law of any state in reliance upon the exemptions contained in such state securities law.

20.03 **Nature of Investment**. Each of the Partners does hereby acknowledge that, prior to his or her execution of this Agreement, he or she received a copy of this Agreement and that he or she has examined this document or caused this document to be examined by his or her representative or attorney.

20.04 Valid Existence. Each Partner represents and warrants to the Partnership and each other Partner that:

(a) if the Partner is a corporation, it is duly organized, validly existing, and in good standing under the laws of the state of its incorporation or is duly qualified and in good standing as a foreign corporation in the jurisdiction of its principal place of business (if not incorporated therein), and if its state of incorporation is Texas, it is duly organized, validly existing, and in good standing under the laws of the State of Texas;

(b) if that Partner is a partnership, trust, or other entity, it is duly formed, validly existing, and (if applicable) in good standing in the jurisdiction of its principal place of business (if not formed therein) and, if a General Partner in the State of Texas, and the representations and warranties in Section 20.04(a) or (b) of this Agreement, as applicable, are true and correct with respect to each partner (other than limited partners), trustee, or other member thereof;

(c) Partner has full corporate, partnership, trust or other applicable power and authority to enter into this Agreement and to perform its obligations hereunder and all necessary actions by the board of directors, shareholders, partners, beneficiaries, or other persons necessary for the due authorization, execution, delivery, and performance of this Agreement by that Partner have been duly taken;

(d) Partner has duly executed and delivered this Agreement; and

(e) Partner's authorization, execution, delivery, and performance of this Agreement do not conflict with any other agreement or arrangement to which that Partner is a party or by which it is bound.

Article XXI
Miscellaneous

21.01 Applicable Laws. This Agreement, and its application or interpretation, shall be governed exclusively by its terms and construed in accordance with the substantive federal laws of the United States and by the laws of the State of Texas, including the Texas conflicts of laws rules.

21.02 Cumulative Remedies. Each party to this Agreement is entitled to all remedies provided by this Agreement and in law or equity. These remedies are cumulative and the use of one right or remedy by any party does not preclude or waive the right to use any or all other remedies.

21.03 Counterparts. This Agreement may be executed in any number of counterparts with the same effect as if all parties had all signed the same document. All counterparts shall be construed together and shall constitute one agreement.

21.04 Entire Agreement. This Agreement shall constitute the entire contract between the parties. There are no other or further agreements outstanding not specifically mentioned in this Agreement. However, the parties may amend and supplement this Agreement in writing, from time to time, in a manner and to the extent provided by the terms of this Agreement, including but not limited to the terms set out in Article XIX.

21.05 Severance of Invalid Provisions. In case any one or more of the sentences or provisions contained in this Agreement are subsequently determined to be invalid, illegal, or unenforceable in any respect, that invalidity or unenforceability does not destroy the basis of the bargain among the Partners as expressed in this Agreement. The invalid sentence or provision shall be deemed severed from the remainder of the Agreement and the validity, legality, and enforceability of the remainder of this Agreement shall not be affected or impaired in any way.

21.06 Signature Pages. Each Partner authorized the General Partner to attach an executed signature page to this Agreement.

21.07 Attorney Fees. If any litigation is initiated by any Partner against another Partner relating to this Agreement or its subject matter, the Partner prevailing in such litigation shall be entitled to recover, in addition to all damages allowed by law and other relief, all court costs and reasonable attorney's fees incurred in connection with the litigation.

21.08 Other Instruments. The parties hereto covenant and agree that they will execute such other and further instruments and documents as are or may become necessary or convenient to effectuate and carry out the Partnership created by this Agreement.

21.09 Headings. The headings used in this Agreement are used for administrative purposes only and do not constitute matter to be considered in construing the terms of this Agreement.

21.10 Parties Bound. This Agreement shall be binding upon and inure to the benefit of the parties hereto and their respective heirs, executors, administrators, legal representatives, successors, and assigns where permitted by this Agreement.

21.11 Prior Agreements Superseded. This Agreement supersedes any prior understandings or agreements between the parties respecting the within subject matter.

21.12 Gender. Wherever the context shall so require, all words herein in the male gender shall be deemed to include the female or neuter gender, all words in the neuter gender shall be deemed to include the male and female gender, all singular words shall include the plural, and all plural words shall include the singular.

[Signature page will follow.]

EXECUTED AND DATED as follows:

GENERAL PARTNER:

Ferguson Family GP, L.L.C.,
A Texas limited liability company

By:_____
      James "Pa" Ferguson, Manager

Being the sole Manager of Ferguson
Family GP, L.L.C.

Address:
123 Capitol Way
Austin, Texas 78701

Date: March 15, 2013

LIMITED PARTNERS:

_____
James "Pa" Ferguson

Address:
123 Capitol Way
Austin, Texas 78701

Date: March 15, 2013

_____
Miriam A. "Ma" Ferguson

Address:
123 Capitol Way
Austin, Texas 78701

Date: March 15, 2013

STATE OF TEXAS   §
            §
COUNTY OF TARRANT §

   BEFORE ME, the undersigned authority, a notary public in and for said county and state, on this day personally appeared James "Pa" Ferguson, known to me to be the person and manager whose name is subscribed to the foregoing instrument and acknowledged to me that the same was executed as an act of Ferguson Family GP, L.L.C., and that he executed the same for the purposes and considerations therein expressed, and in the capacities therein stated.

   GIVEN UNDER MY HAND AND SEAL OF OFFICE this 15th day of March, 2013.

           _____
           NOTARY PUBLIC, STATE OF TEXAS

STATE OF TEXAS   §
            §
COUNTY OF TARRANT §

   BEFORE ME, the undersigned authority, a notary public in and for said county and state, on this day personally appeared James "Pa" Ferguson, known to me to be the person whose name is subscribed to the foregoing instrument and acknowledged to me that the same was executed for the purposes and considerations therein expressed.

   GIVEN UNDER MY HAND AND SEAL OF OFFICE this 15th day of March, 2013.

           _____
           NOTARY PUBLIC, STATE OF TEXAS

STATE OF TEXAS   §
                                 §
COUNTY OF TARRANT   §

     BEFORE ME, the undersigned authority, a notary public in and for said county and state, on this day personally appeared Miriam A. "Ma" Ferguson, known to me to be the person whose name is subscribed to the foregoing instrument and acknowledged to me that the same was executed for the purposes and considerations therein expressed.

     GIVEN UNDER MY HAND AND SEAL OF OFFICE this 15th day of March, 2013.

                                     _____
                                     NOTARY PUBLIC, STATE OF TEXAS

Exhibit A

Initial Partners' Capital Contributions

GENERAL PARTNER	CONTRIBUTION
Ferguson Family GP, L.L.C.	$10.00

LIMITED PARTNERS	CONTRIBUTION
James "Pa" Ferguson	$495.00
Miriam A. "Ma" Ferguson	$495.00

Exhibit B

Initial Partners' Percentage Interest

GENERAL PARTNER	PERCENTAGE INTEREST
Ferguson Family GP, L.L.C., General Partner	1%

LIMITED PARTNERS	PERCENTAGE INTEREST
James "Pa" Ferguson, Limited Partner	49.5%
Miriam A. "Ma" Ferguson, Limited Partner	49.5%

Exhibit C

JOINDER AGREEMENT

This Joinder Agreement (this "Joinder") to Limited Partnership Agreement of Ferguson Family Limited Partnership dated March 15, 2013, by, between and among Ferguson Family Limited Partnership (the "Partnership"), Ferguson Family GP, L.L.C., a Texas limited liability company (the "GP"), James "Pa" Ferguson and Miriam A. "Ma" Ferguson, as amended from time to time (the "Partnership Agreement"), is made and entered into effective _____, 20___ by and among the Partnership and the undersigned (the "Joining Limited Partner"). Capitalized terms used and not defined herein shall have the meanings ascribed to such terms in the Partnership Agreement.

Whereas, the undersigned is acquiring a ____% Partnership Interest from the Partnership (the "Acquisition"); and

Whereas, the Partnership Agreement requires that the Partnership not issue Partnership Interest until the person acquiring the same execute a counterpart of the Partnership Agreement and become parties to the same contemporaneously with the issuance of such Partnership Interest and that any issuance of Partnership Interest without such execution shall be null and void and of no force or effect; and

Whereas, the undersigned desires to execute this Joinder in order that the Acquisition will comply with the above requirement of the Partnership Agreement.

Now, therefore, in consideration of the foregoing and other good and valuable consideration, the receipt and sufficiency of which are hereby acknowledged, the parties hereto agree as follows:

1.   Agreement to be Bound. The undersigned agrees that, upon the execution of this Joinder, the undersigned shall become a party to the Partnership Agreement and shall be fully bound by, and subject to, all of the covenants, terms and conditions of the Partnership Agreement, and the undersigned shall be deemed a party thereto.

2.   Address for Notices. For the purposes of any and all notices or any other communications related to the Partnership, including, without limitation, under the Partnership Agreement, such notices shall be given in writing addressed to the undersigned at the address set forth below his signature hereto.

3.   Binding Effect. This Joinder shall be binding upon and shall inure to the benefit of, and be enforceable by, the Partnership, the other parties to the Partnership Agreement and the undersigned and their respective permitted heirs, personal representatives, successors and assigns.

4.   Severability. If any provision of this Joinder (or any portion thereof) or the application of any such provision (or any portion thereof) to any person, entity or circumstance shall be held invalid, illegal or unenforceable in any respect, such invalidity, illegality or unenforceability shall not affect any other provision hereof (or the remaining portion thereof) or the application of such provision to any other person, entity or circumstance. Upon such determination that any provision of this Joinder (or any portion thereof) or the application of any such provision (or any

165

portion thereof) to any person, entity or circumstance is invalid, illegal or unenforceable, the parties hereto shall negotiate in good faith to modify this Joinder so as to effect the original intent of the parties hereto as closely as possible in an acceptable manner to the end that the transactions contemplated hereby are fulfilled to the extent possible.

     5.   Amendments. This Joinder may be modified or amended only with the written consent of the Partnership and the undersigned, except that modifications, amendments, waivers, consents or other matters relating to the Partnership, including, without limitation, the Certificate of Formation and/or the Partnership Agreement shall not be deemed modifications or amendments of this Joinder.

     6.   Interpretation. The parties acknowledge that they each were permitted to employ counsel of her/his/its choice in the drafting and interpretation of this Joinder. Accordingly, the rule of construction against the drafter shall not apply in the interpretation and/or enforcement hereof or in connection herewith. Headings used herein are for convenience of the parties only and shall not be used in the interpretation hereof.

     7.   Governing Law, Binding Effect, and Severability. This Joinder shall be enforced, governed and construed in all respects in accordance with the laws of the State of Texas applicable to contracts executed and performable solely in such state. The parties agree that venue with respect to all matters under or related to this Agreement shall lie exclusively in the federal and/or state courts located in Tarrant County, Texas, to whose jurisdiction the parties irrevocably consent. The undersigned may not assign any of his/her/its rights or obligations hereunder without the prior written consent of the Company, which consent may be withheld in the Company's sole and exclusive discretion, and any assignment in violation of this sentence shall be void. This Joinder and the rights and obligations set forth herein shall be binding upon, and shall inure to the benefit of, the undersigned, the Company and their respective permitted successors and assigns. If any provision of this Joinder, or the application of such provision to any circumstance, shall be invalid under the applicable laws of any jurisdiction, the remainder of this Joinder or the application of such provision to other persons or circumstances or in other jurisdictions shall not be affected thereby.

     8.   Entire Agreement. This Joinder constitutes the entire agreement, and supersedes all prior agreements and/or understandings, among the parties hereto with respect to the subject matter hereof. The undersigned hereto shall use its commercially reasonable efforts to do and perform or cause to be done and performed all such further acts and things and shall execute and deliver all such other agreements, certificates, instruments or documents as the Company may request, from time to time, in order to carry out the intents and purposes of this Joinder and to consummate the transactions contemplated hereby.

     9.   Counterparts. This Joinder may be executed in separate counterparts, each of which when so executed shall be deemed to be an original and all of which taken together shall constitute one and the same agreement. Delivery of an executed counterpart of a signature page of this Joinder by facsimile or other electronic image scan shall be effective as delivery of a manually executed counterpart of this Joinder.

In witness whereof, the parties hereto have executed this Joinder as of the date first above written.

UNDERSIGNED:

By:_____

Address:

_____
_____

PARTNERSHIP:

GENERAL PARTNER:

Ferguson Family GP, L.L.C.,
a Texas limited liability company

By:_____
    James "Pa" Ferguson, Manager

Being the Sole Manager of Ferguson
Family GP, L.L.C.

Address:

_____
_____

STATE OF TEXAS   §
                             §
COUNTY OF _____   §

    This instrument was acknowledged before me effective the _____ day of _____, _____, by _____.

_____
NOTARY PUBLIC, STATE OF TEXAS

Appendix B

COMPANY AGREEMENT
OF
GREAT EXPECTATIONS, LLC
A TEXAS LIMITED LIABILITY COMPANY

NOTICE: THE SECURITIES EVIDENCED BY THIS AGREEMENT HAVE NOT BEEN REGISTERED UNDER THE SECURITIES ACT OF 1933, AS AMENDED (THE "*SECURITIES ACT*") OR UNDER ANY APPLICABLE STATE SECURITIES LAWS. SUCH SECURITIES HAVE BEEN ACQUIRED FOR INVESTMENT PURPOSES ONLY AND MAY NOT BE SOLD, TRANSFERRED, OR OFFERED FOR SALE UNTIL SUCH INTERESTS ARE REGISTERED UNDER THE SECURITIES ACT OR OF THE STATE OF TEXAS OR UNLESS EXEMPTION(S) FROM THE REGISTRATION REQUIREMENTS OF SUCH ACTS ARE THEN APPLICABLE TO SUCH OFFER OR SALE TO THE SATISFACTION OF THE OPINION OF COUNSEL FOR COMAPNY, AND THE PROVISIONS OF THIS AGREEMENT ARE SATISFIED.

This Company Agreement of GREAT EXPECTATIONS, LLC (this "*Agreement*"), dated as of March 15, 2013, is adopted by the Managers (as defined in Section 5.01) and executed and agreed to for good and valuable consideration, the receipt and sufficiency of which is hereby acknowledged, by the Members (as defined in Section 2.01).

Article I
Organization

1.01. **Formation.** GREAT EXPECTATIONS, LLC (the "*Company*") has been organized as a Texas limited liability company. The Company exists as of the date of the filing of Certificate of Formation (the "*Certificate*") under and pursuant to the Texas Limited Liability Company Law, as that term is defined in Section 1.008(e) of the Texas Business Organization Code, (the "*TLLCL*") (the "*Effective Date*"). No business shall be conducted by the Company or on behalf of the Company prior to the Effective Date.

1.02. **Name.** The name of the Company is "GREAT EXPECTATIONS, LLC" and all Company business must be conducted in that name or such other names that may be selected by the Managers and that comply with the TLLCL.

1.03. **Registered Office; Registered Agent; Offices.** The registered office and registered agent of the Company in the State of Texas shall be as specified in the Certificate or as designated by the Managers in the manner provided by the TLLCL. The offices of the Company shall be at such places as the Managers may designate, which need not be in the state of Texas.

1.04. **Purposes.** The purposes of the Company are those set forth in the Certificate.

1.05. **Foreign Qualification.** Prior to the Company's conducting business in any jurisdiction other than Texas, the Managers shall cause the Company to comply with all requirements necessary to qualify the Company as a foreign limited liability company in that jurisdiction.

1.06. Term of Existence. The Company commenced on the date the Secretary of State of the State of Texas filed the Certificate for the Company and shall continue in existence perpetually or until such earlier time as this Agreement may specify.

1.07. Non-Partnership Entity. The Members intend that the Company not be deemed a partnership, limited partnership, or joint venture, and that no Member or Manager be a partner or joint venturer of any other Member or Manager, for any purposes other than applicable tax laws, and this Agreement may not be construed to suggest otherwise. To this end, the Company has, or will have, made appropriate filings with the Secretary of State of the State of Texas, purposefully and lawfully establishing the Company as a limited liability company under the laws of the State of Texas.

Article II
Membership; Dispositions of Interests

2.01. Members; Sharing Ratios. As used in this Agreement, the term *"Person"* refers to an individual or entity. The Members of the Company are the individuals or entities (by personal representative) executing this Agreement as of the date hereof as Members and each Person that is hereafter admitted to the Company as a Member in accordance with this Agreement (*"Members"*). If a Member shall have made a Disposition (as defined in Section 2.02) of all or any portion of its Membership Interest (as defined in Section 2.02) but shall have retained any rights therein, then solely with respect to the Membership Interest (or portion thereof) so disposed, all references to *"Member"* that appear in Article 4 and Section 8.02(b) shall be deemed to refer to the assignee of such Membership Interest. All other references to *"Member"* shall refer to the assignor unless or until the assignee becomes a Member as provided below. The initial Sharing Ratio and Commitment (herein so called) of each initial Member is set forth on Exhibit A attached hereto and incorporated herein by reference.

2.02. Dispositions of Membership Interests. A Member may not make a sale, assignment, transfer, conveyance, gift, exchange, or other disposition, whether voluntarily, involuntarily, or by operation of law (each, a *"Disposition"*), of all or any portion of its rights or interest in the Company (*"Membership Interest"*), other than a Disposition resulting from the death of such Member, except with the written consent of a majority of the Managers and a Member Majority (as defined in Section 5.07) calculated without including the Member desiring to make such Disposition.

(a)   Rights of Assignees to Become Members.   Any Person to whom a Membership Interest is Disposed, including one who is assigned a Membership Interest as a result of the death of a Member (any *"Assignee"*), may be admitted to the Company as a Member only with the unanimous written consent of the Members and Managers; and (without limiting the generality of Section 5.02) each Manager's or Member's consent may be given or withheld in its sole and absolute discretion, with or without cause, and subject to such conditions as it shall deem appropriate. Unless or until the Assignee becomes a Member as provided in this Agreement, the disposing Member continues to be a Member. Notwithstanding the foregoing, no Assignee of all or any portion of a Membership Interest shall have the right to become a Member unless all of the following occur:

(i)   the Member making such Disposition and the Assignee shall furnish the Managers with an instrument of Disposition stating the disposing Member's intention that the Assignee hold the Membership interest or portion thereof in his or her own right;

(ii)   the Assignee ratifies this Agreement;

(iii)   the disposing Member provides a legal opinion satisfactory to counsel for the Company that the Disposition complies with applicable federal and state securities laws;

(iv)   the disposing Member provides a legal opinion that the Disposition will not result in the Company's termination under Section 708 of the Internal Revenue Code of 1986 (as amended from time to time, the "*Code*");

(v)   the disposing Member or Assignee pays any reasonable expenses in connection with the Disposition; and

(vi)   the Disposition is received by the Company and recorded on the books of the Company.

(b)   <u>Invalid Dispositions</u>. Any attempted Disposition of all or any portion of a Membership Interest, other than in strict accordance with this Section 2.02, shall be null and void *ab initio*.

(i)   *Nonrecognition of an Unauthorized Disposition.* The Company will not be required to recognize the interest of any Assignee who has obtained a purported Membership Interest as the result of a Disposition that is not authorized by this Agreement. If there is a doubt as to ownership of a Membership Interest or as to who is entitled to a cash distribution or allocation or other property, the Managers may accumulate cash or allocations or other property until the issue is resolved to the satisfaction of a majority of the Managers.

(ii)   *Acquisition of an Interest Conveyed to Another Without Authority.* If any Person acquires the Membership Interest or becomes an Assignee as the result of an order of a court which the Company is required by law to recognize, or if a Member makes an unauthorized Disposition of a Membership Interest, which the Company is required by law (and by order of a court) to recognize, the Company will have the unilateral option to acquire the interest of the Assignee, or any fraction or part thereof, upon the following terms and conditions:

a.   The Company will have the option to acquire the interest by giving written notice to the Assignee of its intent to purchase within ninety (90) days after the date it is finally determined that the Company is required to recognize the transfer or assignment.

b.   The valuation date for the determination of the purchase price of the interest will be the first day of the month following the month in which notice is delivered.

c.   Unless the Company and the Assignee agree otherwise, the purchase price for the interest, or any fraction to be acquired by the Company, shall be its fair market value as determined by an appraisal, including any applicable discount for a minority interest. This appraisal shall be performed by a qualified appraiser to be selected by agreement of the Company and the Assignee. If the parties cannot agree on an appraiser, each party shall select his own appraiser and the selected appraisers shall agree on a third appraiser, which third appraiser shall conduct the appraisal. If the appraisers cannot agree on a third appraiser or if such third appraiser refuses to conduct the appraisal, one may be appointed by a court of competent jurisdiction.

d.   Closing of the sale will occur at the principal office or registered office of the Company, at the Company's election, at ten o'clock a.m. (10:00 a.m.) Central Time on the first Tuesday of the month following the month in which the appraisal is rendered.

e.   In order to reduce the burden upon the resources of the Company, the Company will have the option, to be exercised in writing delivered at or before closing, to pay its purchase money obligation in fifteen (15) equal annual installments (or the remaining term of the Company if less than fifteen (15) years) with interest at a rate per annum equal to the lesser of (1) the Wall Street Journal prime rate as quoted in the money rate section of the Wall Street Journal on the date of closing or (2) the maximum rate permitted by applicable law. This rate will be adjusted January 1 of the year immediately following the closing and every January 1 subsequent thereto to be the lesser of (1) the Wall Street Journal prime rate as quoted in the money rate section of the Wall Street Journal on that January 1 or (2) the maximum rate permitted by applicable law. The first installment of principal, with interest, will be due and payable on the first day of the calendar year following closing, and subsequent annual installments, with accrued interest, will be due and payable on the first day of each succeeding calendar year until the entire amount of the obligation is paid. The Company will have the right to prepay all or any part of the purchase money obligation at any time without penalty.

f.   By consent of a Member Majority, calculated without inclusion of the Member whose interest is to be acquired, but only if there is more than one Member, the Managers may assign all or part of the Company's option to purchase to one or more of the remaining Members and, when done, any rights or obligations imposed upon the Company will instead become, by substitution, the rights and obligations of the Member(s) who are Assignees.

g.   Neither the Assignee of an unauthorized Disposition nor the Member causing the Disposition will have the right to vote on Company matters during the prescribed option period or, if the option to purchase is timely exercised, until the sale is closed.

2.03.   Encumbrances of Membership Interests. A Member may not pledge, mortgage, subject to a security interest or lien, or otherwise encumber, whether voluntarily, involuntarily, or by operation of law, all or any portion of its Membership Interest without the written consent of the

Managers and a Member Majority calculated without including the Member desiring to make such encumbrance.

2.04. Creation of Additional Membership Interests. Additional Membership Interests may be created and issued to existing Members or to other persons or entities (each, a "*Person*"), and such other Persons may be admitted to the Company as Members, at the direction of the Managers and with the unanimous written consent of the Members, on such terms and conditions, and with such Sharing Ratios and Commitments, as the Managers and such Member Majority may determine at the time of admission. The Managers may reflect the admission of any new Members or the creation of any new class or group of Member in an amendment to this Agreement that need be executed only by the Managers.

2.05. Voluntary Disassociation. A Member does not have the right or power to withdraw from the Company.

2.06. Information. In addition to the other rights specifically set forth in this Agreement, each Member and each Assignee is entitled to all information to which that Member or Assignee is entitled to have access pursuant to Sections 3.151 (excluding 3.151(a)(2) except as otherwise provided in this Agreement) and 101.501 of the TLLCL under the circumstances and subject to the conditions therein stated.

2.07. Liability to Third Parties. No Member or Manager shall be liable for the debts, obligations, or liabilities of the Company, including under a judgment, decree or order of a court.

2.08. Expulsion. A Member may not be expelled from the Company.

2.09. Spouses of Members. Spouses of Members do not become Members as a result of such marital relationship.

Article III
Capital Contributions; Company Property

3.01. Initial Contributions. Contemporaneously with the execution by such Member of this Agreement, each Member shall contribute to the capital of the Company ("*Capital Contributions*") the amount elected for that Member in Exhibit A.

3.02. Subsequent Contributions. Without creating any rights in favor of any third party, each Member shall contribute to the Company, in cash, on or before the date specified as hereinafter described, that Member's Sharing Ratio of all monies that in the judgment of a majority of the Managers are necessary to enable the Company to cause the assets of the Company to be properly operated and maintained and to discharge its costs, expenses, obligations, and liabilities; provided, however, that a Member is not obligated to contribute a total amount that, when added to all Capital Contributions that Member previously has made pursuant to Section 3.01 or this Section 3.02, exceeds that Member's Commitment as set out in Exhibit A.

3.03. Failure to Contribute.

(a) If a Member does not contribute, within ten (10) days of the date required, all or any portion of a Capital Contribution that Member is required to make as provided in this Agreement, a majority of the Managers (calculated without including a Manager that is also the Delinquent Member) may, following forty-five (45) days advanced written notice to such Member of the same and provided that such contribution is not made within said forty-five (45) days, cause the Company to exercise, on notice to that Member (the "***Delinquent Member***"), one or more of the following remedies:

(i) taking such action (including court proceedings), at the cost and expense of the Delinquent Member, as the Managers may deem appropriate to obtain payment by the Delinquent Member of the portion of the Delinquent Member's Capital Contribution that is in default, together with interest thereon from the date that the Capital Contribution was due, at a rate per annum equal to the maximum rate permitted by applicable law;

(ii) exercising the rights of a secured party under the Uniform Commercial Code of the State of Texas, as more fully set forth in Section 3.03(b); or

(iii) exercising any other rights and remedies available at law or in equity.

(b) Each Member grants to the Company, as security for the payment of all Capital Contributions that Member has agreed to make, a security interest in and a general lien on its Membership Interest and the proceeds thereof, as provided for under the Uniform Commercial Code of the State of Texas. On any default in the payment of a Capital Contribution (following notice as provided above), the Company is entitled to all the rights and remedies of a secured party under the Uniform Commercial Code of the State of Texas with respect to the security interest granted in this Section 3.03(b). Each Member shall execute and deliver to the Company all financing statements and other instruments that the Managers may request to affect and carry out the preceding provisions of this Section 3.03(b). At the option of the Managers, this Agreement or a carbon, photographic, or other copy hereof may serve as a financing statement.

3.04. Return of Contributions. A Member is not entitled to the return of any part of its Capital Contributions or to be paid interest in respect of either its capital account or its Capital Contributions. An unrepaid Capital Contribution is not a liability of the Company or of any Member. No Member is required to contribute or to lend any cash or property to the Company to enable the Company to return any other Member's Capital Contributions.

3.05. Loans by Members. If the Company does not have sufficient cash to pay its obligations, any Member(s), with the written consent of the Managers, may advance all or part of the needed funds to or on behalf of the Company, at such interest rate and on such other terms as such Member and the Managers may agree. An advance described in this Section 3.05 constitutes a loan from the Member to the Company and is not a Capital Contribution.

3.06. Title to Company Property. Legal title to all property of the Company shall be held and conveyed in the name of the Company. No Manager or Member shall have any personal interest in the property of the Company. For all purposes, however, a Membership Interest in the Company shall be the personal property of the Person bearing such interest.

Article IV
Distributions and Allocations

4.01. Distributions. At such time as determined by the Managers, Net Cash Flow (as defined in this Section 4.01) for each fiscal year (or such shorter period for which the distribution is made) shall be distributed to the Members in proportion to their Sharing Ratios. *"Net Cash Flow"* shall include all cash funds derived by the Company (including interest received on reserves, borrowings, and capital transactions), without reduction for any non-cash charges, but reduced by the amount of cash funds used to pay current operating expenses, debt payments, capital improvements, replacements, and to establish reasonable reserves for future expenses and costs as determined by a majority of the Managers should the Managers desire, in their sole discretion, to have such reserves.

4.02. Allocations. Except as may be required by Code Section 704(c) and Treasury Regulation Section 1.704-3, all items of income, gain, loss, deduction, and credit of the Company shall be allocated to the Members in accordance with their Sharing Ratios.

Article V
Management

5.01. Management by Managers.

(a)   Subject to the provisions of Section 5.02 of this Agreement, the powers of the Company shall be exercised by or under the authority of, and the business and affairs of the Company shall be managed under the direction of, managers of the Company (*"Managers"*). No Member in its capacity as a Member has the right, power, or authority to act for or on behalf of the Company, to do any act that would be binding on the Company, or to incur any expenditure on behalf of the Company.

(b)   In managing the business and affairs of the Company and exercising its powers, the Managers shall act collectively (i) through resolutions adopted at meetings and in written consents pursuant to Sections 5.04 and 5.08; and (ii) through committees and individual Managers to which authorities and duties have been delegated pursuant to Section 5.05. No Manager has the right, power, or authority to act for or on behalf of the Company, to do any act that would be binding on the Company, or to incur any expenditure on behalf of the Company, except those delegated in accordance with the provisions of this Agreement. Decisions or actions taken by the Managers in accordance with this Agreement, including, but not limited to, this Section 5.01 and Section 5.02, shall constitute decisions or actions by the Company and shall be binding on each Manager, Member, Officer (as defined in Section 5.09), and employee of the Company.

5.02. Decisions Requiring Member Consent. Notwithstanding any power or authority granted the Managers under the TLLCL, the Certificate or this Agreement, the Managers may not make any decision or take any action for which the consent of a Member Majority or other consent of the Members is expressly required by the Certificate or this Agreement. Each Member may, with respect to any vote, consent, or approval that it is entitled to grant pursuant to this Agreement, grant or withhold such vote, consent, or approval in its sole and absolute discretion, with or without cause, and subject to such conditions as it shall deem appropriate. This Section 5.02 shall supersede Section 101.356(b) of the TLLCL.

5.03. Selection of Managers. The number of Managers of the Company shall be the number set forth in the Certificate as the number of initial Managers, unless such number is changed by a unanimous written consent of the Members. The initial Managers of the Company shall be the Persons named in the Certificate as the initial Managers. Managers need not be Members or residents of the State of Texas. Each Manager (whether an initial or a successor Manager) shall cease to be a Manager upon the earliest to occur of the following events: (a) such Manager shall engage in gross negligence, fraud, bad faith, or willful misconduct in the performance of his duties as a Manager and, as a result thereof, shall be removed by consent of a Member Majority (not including a Member that is such Manager) at a meeting of the Members called for that purpose; (b) such Manager shall resign as a Manager, by giving written notice of such resignation to the Members; (c) such Manager shall die, terminate (unless its business is continued without the commencement of liquidation or winding up), or become bankrupt; for purposes of this Subsection (c) bankrupt shall include taking or acquiescing in the taking, of any action seeking relief under, or advantage of, any applicable debtor relief, liquidation, receivership, conservatorship, bankruptcy, moratorium, rearrangement, insolvency, reorganization or similar law affecting the rights or remedies of creditors generally, as in effect from time to time; and for the purpose of this definition, the term "acquiescing" shall include, without limitation, the failure to file, within ten (10) days after its entry, a petition, answer, or motion to vacate or to discharge any order, judgment, or decree providing for any relief under any such law; or (d) such Manager is removed, with or without cause, by consent of a Member Majority (including a Member that is such Manager). Any vacancy in any Manager position may be filled by consent of a Member Majority at a meeting of the Members called for that purpose, or by a majority of the remaining Managers, though less than a quorum of the Managers.

5.04. Meetings of Managers. Regular meetings of the Managers may be held on such dates and at such times as shall be determined by the Managers, with written notice of the establishment of such regular meetings subsequently scheduled being given to each Manager that was not present at the meeting at which it was scheduled. Special meetings of the Managers may be called by any Manager by written notice thereof that is delivered to each other Manager at least 24 hours prior to such meeting and specifying the place and time of such meeting. Neither the business to be transacted at such special meeting nor the purpose of such special meeting need be specified in the notice (or waiver of notice) thereof. Unless otherwise expressly provided in this Agreement, at any meeting of the Managers, an act of the Managers shall be an act in which the Managers act unanimously. The provisions of this Section 5.04 shall be inapplicable at any time that there is only one Manager.

5.05. Committees of Managers; Delegation of Authority to Individual Managers. The Managers may designate one or more committees, each of which shall be comprised of one or more of the Managers, and may designate one or more of the Managers as alternate members of any committee. Except for matters that cannot be delegated to such a committee pursuant to the TLLCL, any such committee, to the extent provided in the resolution establishing it, shall have and may exercise all of the authority that may be exercised as granted by the Managers. Regular and special meetings of such committee shall be held in the manner designated by the Managers or, if not so designated, by such committee. The Managers may dissolve any committee at any time. In addition, the Managers may delegate to one or more Managers such authority and duties, and assign to them such titles, as the Managers may deem advisable. Any such delegation may be revoked at any time by the Managers.

5.06. Compensation of Manager. The Managers shall receive such compensation, if any, for their services as may be designated by a Member Majority, and absent such designation, the Managers shall not be entitled to compensation of any kind for serving as a Manager. In addition, the Managers shall be entitled to be reimbursed for reasonable and necessary out-of-pocket costs and expenses incurred in the course of their service hereunder in the reasonable discretion of a Member Majority.

5.07. Meetings of Members. An annual meeting of the Members for the transaction of such business as may properly come before the meeting shall be held on such date and at such time as the Managers shall specify in a written notice of the meeting, which shall be delivered to each Member at least twenty (20) days prior to such meeting. Special meetings of the Members may be called by the Managers or by Members having among them at least ten percent (10%) of the Sharing Ratios of all Members. Any such meeting shall be held on such date and at such time as the Person calling such meeting shall specify in the notice of the meeting, which shall be delivered to each Member at least ten (10) days prior to such meeting. Only business within the purpose or purposes described in the notice (or waiver thereof) for such meeting may be conducted at such meeting. Unless otherwise expressly provided in this Agreement, at any meeting of the Members, Members holding among them at least fifty-one percent (51%) of all Sharing Ratios (a "*Member Majority*"), represented either in person or by proxy, shall constitute a quorum for the transaction of business, and an act of a Member Majority shall be the act of the Members.

5.08. Provisions Applicable to All Meetings. In connection with any meeting of the Managers, Members, or any committee of the Managers, the following provisions shall apply:

(a)   Place of Meeting. Any such meeting shall be held at the principal place of business of the Company, unless the notice of such meeting (or resolution of the Managers or committee, as applicable) specifies a different place, which need not be in the State of Texas, but must be in the State of Texas if so requested in any form, whether written, oral, or otherwise, by a Member Majority.

(b)   Waiver of Notice through Attendance. Attendance of a Person at such meeting (including pursuant to Section 5.08(e)) shall constitute a waiver of notice of such meeting,

177

except where such Person attends the meeting for the express purpose of objecting to the transaction of any business on the ground that the meeting is not lawfully called or convened.

(c)   Proxies. A Person may vote at such meeting by a written proxy executed by that Person and delivered to another Manager, Member, or member of the committee, as applicable. A proxy shall be revocable unless it is stated to be irrevocable and coupled with an interest as required by law.

(d)   Action by Written Consent. Any action required or permitted to be taken at such a meeting may be taken without a meeting, without prior notice, and without a vote if a consent or consents in writing, setting forth the action so taken, is signed by the Managers, Members, or members of the committee, as applicable, having not fewer than the minimum number of Sharing Ratios or votes that would be necessary to take the action at a meeting at which all Members, Managers, or members of the committee, as applicable, entitled to vote on the action were present and voted. Any such written consent must be dated, signed and delivered in the manner required by, and shall be effective for the period specified by the TLLCL. Prompt notice of the taking of any action by Members without a meeting by less than unanimous written consent shall be given to those Members who did not consent in writing to the action.

(e)   Meetings by Telephone. Managers, Members, or members of the committee, as applicable, may participate in and hold such meeting by means of conference telephone, videoconference, or similar communications equipment by means of which all Persons participating in the meeting can hear each other.

5.09. Officers. The Managers may designate one or more Persons to be officers of the Company ("*Officers*"), and any Officers so designated shall have such title, authorities, duties, and salaries as the Managers may delegate to them. Any Officer may be removed as such, either with or without cause, by the Managers.

5.10. Limitations on Liability of Managers and Officers. A Manager or Officer shall be liable to the Company and the other Members for acts or omissions in the management of the Company only in the case of gross negligence, willful misconduct, or material breach of these regulations by such Manager or Officer; but a Manager or Officer shall not be liable to the Company or any other Member for any other acts or omissions, including the negligence, strict liability, or other fault or responsibility (short of gross negligence, willful misconduct, or breach of these regulations) by such Manager or Officer.

5.11. Other and Competing Activities. Subject to the other express provisions of this Agreement and any other agreements or commitments, each Member, Manager, Officer, or affiliate thereof may engage in and possess interests in other business ventures of any and every type and description, independently or with others, including ones in competition with the Company, with no obligation to offer to the Company or any other Member, Manager, or Officer the right to participate therein. The Company may transact business with any Member, Manager, Officer, or Affiliate thereof, provided the terms of those transactions are no less favorable than those the Company could obtain from unrelated third parties.

5.12.   Indemnification of Managers and Officers. The Company shall indemnify, defend, protect and hold harmless each Manager and each Officer from and against all actions, suits or proceedings (collectively, "*Proceedings*"), and all other claims, demands, losses, damages, liabilities, judgments, awards, penalties, fines, settlements, costs and expenses (including court costs and reasonable attorneys' fees), arising out of the management of the Company, such Manager's service or status as a Manager or such Officer's service or status as an Officer. **THIS INDEMNITY SHALL APPLY TO MATTERS THAT ARISE OUT OF THE NEGLIGENCE, STRICT LIABILITY OR OTHER FAULT OR RESPONSIBILITY BY SUCH MANAGER OR OFFICER; PROVIDED, HOWEVER, THAT THIS INDEMNITY SHALL NOT APPLY TO MATTERS ARISING OUT OF THE GROSS NEGLIGENCE, WILLFUL MISCONDUCT, FRAUD, BAD FAITH OR BREACH OF THIS AGREEMENT BY SUCH MANAGER OR OFFICER.** The Company, by adoption of a resolution of the Managers, may indemnify an employee or agent of the Company to the same extent and subject to the same conditions under which it may indemnify Managers under this Section 5.12. The Company may purchase and maintain insurance to protect itself and any Manager, Officer, employee or agent of the Company.

Article VI
Taxes

6.01.   Tax Returns. The Company shall prepare and timely file all federal, state, and local tax returns required to be filed by the Company. Each Member shall furnish to the Company all pertinent information in its possession relating to the Company's operations that is necessary to enable the Company's tax returns to be timely prepared and filed. The Company shall deliver a copy of each such return to the Members on or before ten (10) days prior to the due date of any such return, together with such additional information as may be required by the Members in order for the Members to file their individual returns reflecting the Company's operations. The Company shall bear the costs of the preparation and filing of its returns.

6.02.   Annual Accounting and Tax Period. The Company's annual accounting period shall be its taxable year. The Company's taxable year shall be selected by the Managers, subject to the requirements and limitations of the Code.

6.03.   Method of Accounting. The method of accounting of the Company shall be selected by the Managers subject to the requirements and limitations of the Code.

6.04.   Tax Matters Member. The Managers who are Members shall designate one Manager that is a Member to be the "tax matters member" of the Company pursuant to Code Section 6231(a)(7) (the "*Tax Matters Member*"), or, if there is no Manager that is a Member, the Tax Matters Member shall be a Member that has the largest Sharing Ratio at the close of the applicable taxable year. If no Member has a proportionally greater Sharing Ratio, then the Tax Matters Member shall be a Member delegated such authority by a majority of the Managers. The Tax Matters Member shall take such action as may be necessary to cause to the extent possible each other Member to become a "notice partner" within the meaning of Code Section 6223. The Tax Matters Member shall inform each other Member of all significant matters that may come to its attention in its capacity as Tax Matters Member by giving notice thereof on or before the fifth (5th) business day after becoming aware thereof and, within that time, shall forward to each other Member copies of all significant written communications it may receive in that capacity. The Tax Matters Member shall take no action without the authorization of a Member Majority, other than such action as may be required by applicable law. Any cost or expense incurred by the Tax Matters Member in connection with its duties, including the preparation for or pursuance of administrative or judicial proceedings, shall be paid by the Company.

6.05.   Tax Elections. The Managers shall have the authority to make all Company elections permitted under the Code, including, without limitation, elections of methods regarding cost recovery deductions, depreciation and amortization, and elections under Code Section 754.

Article VII
Books, Records, and Bank Accounts

7.01.   Books and Records. The Managers shall keep or cause to be kept at the principal office of the Company complete and accurate books and records of the Company, supporting documentation of the transactions with respect to the conduct of the Company's business, and minutes of the proceedings of its Managers, Members, and each committee of the Managers. The books and records shall be maintained with respect to accounting matters in accordance with sound accounting practices, and all books and records shall be available at the Company's principal office for examination by any Member or the Member's duly authorized representative at any and all reasonable times during normal business hours.

7.02.   Reports. Within one hundred twenty (120) days after the end of each taxable year of the Company, the Managers will deliver to the Members if requested by the Members at the Company's expense, financial statements setting forth, as of the end of and for that taxable year, a profit and loss statement and a balance sheet of the Company and such other information that, in the judgment of the Managers, is reasonably necessary for the Members to be advised of the results of operations of the Company.

7.03.   Accounts. The Managers shall establish one or more separate bank and investment accounts and arrangements for the Company, which shall be maintained in the Company's name with financial institutions and firms that the Managers determine. The Managers may not commingle the Company's funds with the funds of any Manager or Member.

Article VIII
Winding Up and Termination

8.01.   Events Requiring Wind Up.

(a)   The Company shall wind up its affairs and terminate up on the first to occur of the following events (unless there is revocation or cancellation of such wind up pursuant to Section 101.552 of the TLLCL):

(i)   the consent of a Member Majority;

(ii)   entry of a decree by a court requiring the wind up or dissolution of the Company, rendered under the TLLCL or other law; or

(iii)   the termination of the continued Membership of the last remaining Member, unless within ninety (90) days after such termination, the legal representative or successor of the last remaining Member agrees to continue the Company and to become a Member effective as of the date of such termination or to designate another person who agrees to become a Member as of the date of such termination.

No other event will cause the Company to wind up and terminate.

8.02.   Winding Up and Termination.

(a)   On the occurrence of an event described in Section 8.01(a) (unless there is a revocation or cancellation), the Managers shall act as liquidator or may appoint one or more Members as liquidator. The liquidator shall proceed diligently to wind up the affairs of the Company as provided in the TLLCL. Until final distribution, the liquidator shall continue to operate the Company properties with all of the power and authority of the Managers. The costs of winding up shall be borne as a Company expense.

(b)   Any assets of the Company remaining at the conclusion of the winding-up process shall be distributed among the Members in accordance with their Sharing Ratios. All distributions in kind to the Members shall be made subject to the liability of each distributee for costs, expenses, and liabilities theretofore incurred or for which the Company has committed prior to the date of termination. The distribution of cash or property to a Member in accordance with the provisions of this Section 8.02(b) constitutes a complete return to the Member of its Capital Contributions and a complete distribution to the Member of its Membership Interest and all the Company's property and constitutes a compromise to which all Members have consented within the meaning of Section 101.154 of the TLLCL.

(c)   On completion of such final distribution, the Managers shall file a Certificate of Termination with the Secretary of State of Texas, cancel any other filings made pursuant to Section 1.05, and take such other actions as may be necessary under the TLLCL or otherwise to terminate the existence of the Company.

8.03.   Liquidation. When the Company is liquidated, each Member with a deficit in his or her capital account (whether by virtue of loans, distribution, failure to make an initial contribution, or any other reason) will be obligated to contribute to the capital of the Company an amount of cash equal to the deficit in the capital account balance. The cash must be paid within one hundred eighty (180) days after the date of the liquidation, and the amounts so contributed may be paid to the creditors of the Company or distributed to the other Members in the ratio of the then positive balances in their respective capital accounts.

Article IX
General Provisions

9.01. Offset. Whenever the Company is to pay any sum to any Member, any amounts that Member owes the Company may be deducted from that sum before payment.

9.02. Notices. All notices, requests, or consents under this Agreement shall be (a) in writing, (b) delivered to the recipient in person, by courier or mail or by facsimile, telegram, telex, cablegram, or similar transmission, (c) if to a Member, delivered to such Member at the applicable address on Exhibit A or such other address as that Member may specify by notice to the other Members, (d) if to the Managers or the Company, delivered to the Managers at the following address: 123 Capitol Way, Austin, Texas 78701, and (e) effective only upon actual receipt by such Person. Whenever any notice is required to be given by applicable law, the Certificate, or this Agreement, a written waiver thereof, signed by the Person entitled to notice, whether before or after the time stated therein, shall be deemed equivalent to the giving of such notice.

9.03. Entire Agreement; Prior Agreements Superseded. This Agreement, together with the Certificate, constitutes the entire agreement of the Members relating to the Company and supersedes all prior contracts or agreements with respect to the Company, whether oral or written.

9.04. Effect of Waiver or Consent. A waiver or consent, express or implied, to or of any breach or default by any Person in the performance by that Person of its obligations with respect to the Company is not a consent or waiver to or of any other breach or default in the performance by that Person of the same or any other obligations of that Person with respect to the Company.

9.05. Amendments of Articles and Regulations. The Articles and this Agreement may be amended or restated only with the approval of all of the Members; provided, however, that amendments of the type described in Section 2.04 may be adopted as therein provided.

9.06. Binding Effect. Subject to the restrictions on Dispositions set forth in this Agreement, this Agreement is binding on and inures to the benefit of the Members and their respective heirs, legal representatives, successors, and assigns.

9.07. Governing Law; Venue; Severability. THIS AGREEMENT IS GOVERNED BY AND SHALL BE CONSTRUED IN ACCORDANCE WITH THE LAWS OF THE STATE OF TEXAS (EXCLUDING ITS CONFLICT-OF-LAWS RULES). The Members agree that any and all disputes arising under or related to this Agreement shall be exclusively decided in the federal and state courts of Tarrant County, Texas, to whose jurisdiction each Member irrevocably consents. If any provision of this Agreement or the application thereof to any Person or circumstance is held invalid or unenforceable to any extent, the remainder of this Agreement and the application of that provision to other Persons or circumstances are not affected thereby and that provision shall be enforced to the greatest extent permitted by applicable law.

9.08. Construction. Unless the context requires otherwise: (a) the gender (or lack of gender) of all words used in this Agreement includes the masculine, feminine, and neuter; (b) the word "including" means "including, without limitation", (c) references to Articles and Sections refer to Articles and Sections of this Agreement; (d) references to Exhibits are to the Exhibits attached to this Agreement, each of which is made a part hereof for all purposes; and (e) the headings used in this Agreement are used for administrative purposes only and do not constitute matters to be considered in construing the terms of this Agreement.

9.09. Further Assurances. In connection with this Agreement and the transactions contemplated hereby, each Member shall execute and deliver any additional documents and instruments and perform any additional acts that may be necessary or appropriate to effectuate and perform the provisions of this Agreement and those transactions.

9.10. Counterparts. This Agreement may be executed in any number of counterparts, all of which shall constitute the same instrument.

9.11. Limited Liability. The Members have no personal liability whatsoever, whether to the Company or any creditors of the Company, for any of the debts or losses of the Company beyond their respective Capital Contributions to the Company.

9.12. Signatures. Facsimile signatures or signatures sent by electronic means appearing on this Agreement shall be valid and binding as original signatures.

IN WITNESS WHEREOF, the Company Agreement, to be effective as of the date the Company's existence begins, has been executed by the Members as of the date first set forth above.

MEMBERS:

_____

James "Pa" Ferguson

_____

Miriam A. "Ma" Ferguson

Being all of the Members of the Company.

Exhibit A
Initial Members

James "Pa" Ferguson

123 Capitol Way
Austin, Texas 78701

Initial Capital Contribution:	$500.00
Commitment:	$500.00
Sharing Ratio:	50%
Contribution Due Date:	March 31, 2013

Miriam A. "Ma" Ferguson

123 Capitol Way
Austin, Texas 78701

Initial Capital Contribution:	$500.00
Commitment:	$500.00
Sharing Ratio:	50%
Contribution Due Date:	March 31, 2013

EXHIBIT A TO COMPANY AGREEMENT OF GREAT EXPECTATIONS, LLC

⟶ ACKNOWLEDGMENTS ⟵

Each of the following people made significant contributions to this effort:

My sons, Robert A. Simon and Jeffrey B. Simon, each of whom encouraged me at all times. Robert, a very skilled bankruptcy lawyer, corrected my technical errors regarding bankruptcy and wrote Chapter 9 in its entirety. He was the best man for the job.

My wife, Karen, who completely supported this effort, as she has consistently encouraged me for many years.

To my first editor, Jill Kelly, who brought to her task a great deal of literary knowledge and no knowledge of the world of insolvency. Trying to write in plain, clear language sufficient to pass her editorial test was very important. To my final editors, the talented team at Brown Books Publishing Group in Dallas, who labored consistently, and we hope to good effect, to make this effort both readable and useful.

To the attorneys and staff of Barlow Garsek & Simon, LLP who helped meaningfully in every way. And particularly thanks to Judd Pritchard, an elegant draftsman, who authored the two source documents in the appendix.

To the published authors and scholars whom I know and appreciate only through their publications: J. D. Adkisson, Christopher M. Riser, and Lea Shepard.

⇀ ABOUT THE AUTHOR ⇀

Henry W. Simon Jr., the son and grandson of lawyers, offices primarily in Fort Worth, Texas, with the law firm of Barlow Garsek & Simon, LLP. He is a graduate of Yale University and the Law School of the University of Texas where, along with his partner, he won the annual Moot Court Award resulting from an argument before the Texas Supreme Court. Mr. Simon has been recognized by the "The Best Lawyers in America" and holds the highest distinction awarded by the legal rating firm of Martindale Hubble, that of "AV Preeminent."

He and his wife, Karen L. Simon, have two sons, Robert and Jeffrey, both accomplished lawyers. They are blessed with six grandchildren, ages four through fourteen, not a single one of whom has expressed any desire to become a lawyer.